The Essential Guide to

Practically Perfect Patchwork

Everything You Need to Know to Make Your First Quilt

Michele Morrow Harer

Published by

**krause
publications**

700 East State Street • Iola, WI 54990-0001
715/445-2214 • FAX: 715/445-4087   www.krause.com

Please call or write for our free catalog of publications. To place an order or obtain a free catalog, please call 800-258-0929, or our regular business telephone 715-445-2214.

Library of Congress Catalog Number 2002105751
ISBN 0-87349-440-7

Dedication

To my beloved husband, George, who is my best friend, kindest ally, staunchest supporter, and dearest soul mate. You'll always be the hero of my story.

An old proverb:

"Give a man a fish, and he eats for a day. Teach a man to fish, and he eats for a lifetime."

For quilters:

Give a woman a quilt, and she'll share it with people she loves to keep them warm.

Teach a woman to quilt, and she'll make quilts for: her family, her friends, new babies, strangers who need warmth and comfort, the walls in her home to express her soul, raffles to benefit her favorite charities, art and quilt lovers to make extra money, and contests just to show off a little.

Then she'll teach others to make quilts, so they will have an outlet for their expressions of love.

Acknowledgments

This book is the result of encouragement I received from many people, and I give my heartfelt thanks to each of them.

Thanks to:

Don Gulbrandsen, had he not been so astute and thorough in tracking down the sender of an incomplete e-mail, there probably would be no book; Marny Bryant, who suggested that I write the book; Patti-Jill Stice, my sister, who helped brainstorm the concept of the book and the idea of interjections of whimsy; Becky Herdle, who leads by example, thank you for reading the beginning manuscript and giving me support and direction; Debbie Nagle, my friend, amateur photographer, and multi-talented quilting buddy, who read revision after revision, reasoned explanations and took the photographs for the book. Thanks too, to Linda Hall, friend, quilt artist, and teacher—thank you for sharing your wisdom and experience. Many thanks to friends and students—especially Chong Blind; Kathleen Wagner, Janet Yantch, Ruth Lingg, Sherry Thomas, Lisa Lipp, and Karen Cona. Pam Doell, for giving me the opportunity to discover that in my heart I was a quilt teacher. And last, but certainly not least, my family: Patty and Amy—their encouragement and example as young women of determination taught me how to achieve my goals. Thanks to my son, Andrew, who supported my dreams and believed in my abilities. And thanks to George, the best husband ever for over 37 years, who always had a receptive ear and was a good sport when nightly homemade meals disappeared for a while.

FOREWORD

I feel I've always known and loved quilting, although I was around thirty, married, and had three children when I discovered quilt making in the revival of the '70s. My love of quilting is more than just an enjoyment of the fabrics, colors, or the process. I love everything quilting stands for. I love the history—of being connected to our foremothers through over two centuries of quilting. I love that quilting is a symbol of recycling, of conservation, of making do. I love that quilting is taking common scraps of fabrics and turning them into beautiful works of art. I love the traditions of fellowship that quilting encompasses.

Quilting, to me, is an expression of love, because when you've made a quilt, you realize no one would make one just to pass the time. The work is too compelling, time-consuming, and all involving. A quilt is a warm covering of love for someone you care about. A quilt is an expression of emotions that cannot be put into words. A quilt is a legacy. Besides turning out three wonderful young adults to help make this a better world, my quilts are also one small part of me I can leave behind in memoriam. And at times during my life, quilting was the only thing I did that stayed done!

I have found that quilters are a group of the best people in the world. They are helpful and generous. They share ideas, techniques, their time, their work and (best of all), their fabrics. And that is why I came to write this book. I wish to share with you my love of quilting and the practical methods I have learned that help to ensure the successful completion of a quilt. It is my wish that you, too, will come to love quilting and all it stands for. I hope to infect you with "quilt pox" so that you will enjoy the creativity and personal satisfaction I have found in my beloved hobby. I hope these lessons will be an enjoyable, no-pressure experience for you. I know you will have fun while you learn to make the quilts of a lifetime.

I'd like to share a quote from Texas quilter, Mary White, from a book entitled, *The Quilters—Women and Domestic Art* by Patricia J. Cooper and Norma Bradley Allen. For me, it embodies the truth of quilting, and has brought me comfort through good times and not-so-good times.

"You can't always change things. Sometimes you don't have no control over the way things go. Hail ruins the crops or fire burns you out. And then you're just given so much to work with in a life and you have to do the best you can with what you got. That's what piecing is. The materials is passed on to you or is all you can afford to buy … that's just what's given to you. Your fate. But the way you put them together is your business."[1]

Blessings to you as you embark on this wonderful journey.

Michele

TABLE OF CONTENTS

INTRODUCTION

The Essential Guide to Practically Perfect Patchwork will give you quilt making power. This book is intended to be an introduction into quilting for beginning quilters, and those who have been quilting but want to know how to stitch patchwork blocks with more ease and accuracy. The lessons offer a basic understanding of what constitutes "practically perfect" block construction and includes tips and techniques developed to help you succeed.

Many times my students have told me they were afraid to take a quilt class for fear they would encounter too many rules and face an overly critical examination of their work. Well, there are no quilt police here. If you follow the assembly instructions and use the "tricks" developed to outwit fabric's perversities, your quilt will be as accurate and beautiful as you make it.

There are no bad quilts. There are quilts for different purposes. If you are making a quilt to enter into competition, naturally you will try for excellence. But if you're making a quilt to be loved and used, doing the best you can is enough. If anyone should be so rude as to point out a flaw in your quilt, you can just tell them (as the Amish do) that you left the error in on purpose so that your work wouldn't approach perfection and thus be an affront to God.

In a simple, straightforward way, the patterns included in each lesson will teach all the basic types of seams you will ever need to successfully sew any patchwork block. The blocks are grouped according to the technique or skill to be learned.

Each lesson builds upon the lesson before it, and the whole book is intended to give support at each advancing stage of quilt making. The last four lessons demystify finishing steps and set forth some easy-to-understand tips and techniques that are thoroughly explained and diagrammed so you can use the power of "practically perfect patchwork" to *finish* your quilt. So, if you begin with Lesson 1 and continue through Lesson 10, your quilt will be done!

Whether you choose to make a whole quilt using one block pattern from this workbook or a sampler quilt using many of the patterns, you can finish your quilt using *The Essential Guide to Practically Perfect Patchwork* as your manual through a step-by-step process to success.

The Practically Perfect Bunny

My underlying philosophy as a quilting teacher is to make everything as simple as possible. Over the years, I have accumulated many valuable short cuts and timesaving techniques that make sewing patchwork less difficult, and I want to share them with you.

These helpful hints have multiplied like rabbits, so watch for my bunny helper within each lesson. She will remind you of skills already learned. She will teach you some new tricks. She will even tell you of past mistakes, from which we get our best and longest-lasting instruction.

While our bunny friend will help you hop over the hurdles of patchwork construction, she won't do anything about the dust bunnies that may accumulate in your house while you are sewing. But then, dust bunnies are some of her best friends.

Supply List For Lessons 1 – 6: Making the Blocks

- Template patterns from this book
- X-Acto or red-handled craft knife with size 24 or equally substantial blade
- Paper scissors
- 2-ply, medium weight illustration board or dense cardboard, 1/8" thick
- 5 sheets medium or fine grade sandpaper
- Rubber cement with brush in the cap
- Emery board
- Hard, textured surface cutting board (not a rotary mat)
- .5 mm mechanical pencil with H or HB lead
- 12" or 18" metal ruler with cork backing
- Colored pencils, markers or crayons to color in quilt block diagrams
- Pad of small self-stick notes, 1-1/2" x 2"
- Sewing machine in good working order
- 12/80 machine sewing needles
- Iron and ironing board
- Fabrics for quilt top
- Good fabric scissors
- Long, thin straight pins

- 28 mm rotary cutter
- Rotary cutting mat
- 2 rotary grid rulers: 3" x 18" rectangle, 15" square (You won't need the square until Lesson 7, so watch for sales or ask for it as a special gift. Note: if you buy different sizes of rulers, always choose the same brand to keep your measurements consistent.)
- Temporary fabric marking pens and pencils
- Seam ripper
- Neutral color threads
- Freezer paper
- 120" tape measure

Optional items you may want to add to the list:
- A second smaller mat (less than 12" x 12")
- Rotary point cutter
- Rubber cement "pick-up"
- Thread snips

"Gold and Black Sampler"
57-1/2" X 72-1/2"
made by author

In the Beginning . . .
*L*ESSON *1*

How Patchwork Quilts Came to Be

The quilting tradition in the United States began in the early 1700s as pioneer women searched for ways to keep their families warm in a new land where fiber resources for clothing and blankets were scarce. It was this scarcity of materials that created the serendipitous invention of patchwork quilts as a unique and practical art form. Early quiltmakers, who presumably were untrained in sophisticated design, sewed scraps of fabric together to make bed covers producing many beautiful works of practical art and displaying an inborn talent for pattern, color, harmony, and geometric form.

Quilts were made mostly by women who took pleasure and comfort in quiltmaking as one of the few creative outlets that were allowed to them. Many of the early patchwork patterns reflected the political and moral beliefs their makers cherished but were not allowed to express. I can remember reading about an early 1800s colonial woman, who was the wife of a devout Democrat in favor of an overly strong presidency. She made a beautiful "Whig Rose" quilt for her husband to sleep under. (The Whigs, precursors to the Republican Party, were in favor of strong states rights.) Every night she exerted her silent choice, while her husband slept peacefully under her quilt.

But What Exactly is a Quilt?

A quilt is made of two layers of fabric arranged in sandwich fashion with batting in between. It is held together by thread stitches or ties. Two factors work together to create the beauty of a quilt: 1) the quilt top, the part that is pieced together in interesting combinations of design, color and pattern, and 2) the actual stitching of the three layers together, called quilting, which adds texture and an additional design element to the surface. Piecing and quilting complement each other.

A quilt can be any size, but it must be made of three layers stitched together. Therefore, you can make a quilt for a pillow top, a wall hanging, or your bed. Size is not a restriction.

One-Patch, Two-Patch, Four, Five, Seven, Nine ...

You will discover in your exploration of quilting that block patterns are categorized by the arrangement of the patches. As a teacher, I have found this confusing for the beginner, so don't feel you have to understand and know how to classify blocks. In the future, you can investigate the many fine books written to help you design and draft your own quilts. Two excellent resource books are Dolores Hinson's *A Quilter's Companion*, and Jinny Beyer's *Patchwork Patterns*. Nevertheless, I have categorized many of the blocks in this workbook as an introduction to block classification.

The Sampler

A sampler quilt, also known as an album quilt, is one in which no two blocks are the same. So, how did the "sampler" quilt originate? One common belief is that when a quilter wanted to remember a block she had seen, she made a copy of it out of fabric rather than draw it on paper, another scarce early American commodity. These blocks were her "reference library" from which she could recall patterns for future quilts, although she may not have recorded the block's original name. So, while a block may have started out with the name "Bear's Paw," it may have acquired various other names along the way—"Duck's Foot in the Mud" or "Hand of Friendship"—like stories changing as they pass from person to person. You can see how many traditional patterns came to be known by more than one name. When the quilter who had made a copy of "Bear's Paw" referred back to *her* pattern—blame it on poor memory or that she wanted to put her own spin on the design by naming it differently, somehow the various patterns got renamed and renamed. Later, in pioneer tradition of "waste not, want not," these orphan quilt blocks were sewn together into a bed covering creating the sampler-type quilt we will be making during this series of lessons.

For our purposes, the "Practically Perfect Patchwork" sampler we'll be creating will become your beginning library of patterns to use, and will provide many happy hours of creating beautiful quilts for yourself and loved ones. This book contains all the templates you will need to make over 45 different blocks, so you have the choice of which ones you want to include in your sampler quilt. Later, you may want to use just one block and make a complete quilt with it.

Size Counts

When I made my first sampler quilt, I decided it had to be big enough to cover my queen-sized bed … and, embarrassingly, I am still hand-quilting it. Originally, I embraced the whole hand-quilting tradition and was determined to make my quilt the "old-fashioned way." Well, I do not live an old-fashioned life. My life—and no doubt, yours too—speeds by faster and faster the older I get. When I do get a chance to sit down, I just may fall asleep. That's how I came to develop my theory of "machine quilt where it doesn't show, and hand quilt where it does."

I recommend that you restrict your quilt size to no larger than 60" by 70". You only need to make twelve blocks; with borders, the quilt would be suitable as a topper for a queen-size mattress, or quilt for a smaller bed. Still, it won't be so prohibitively large that you'll lose interest. You will be encouraged as you see your work transformed into a completed quilt. Plus, this smaller size will make it easier to machine quilt your sampler, if you choose.

Planning Ahead

It's very helpful to begin with a definite diagram or scale drawing of the layout and size of the quilt you want to make. Look ahead to Lesson 7, "Make a Blueprint of Your Quilt," for how to draw it. Of course, you are not committed to any layout you might choose now, but it is a good idea to have some sort of target. You may end up making more blocks than required, and want to include them in your quilt, or you may make fewer and finish them into a wall hanging. I've included a few examples of possibilities for you to consider.

Quilt Layout Possibilities and Size Guidelines

THROW: ± 40"x ± 75"
CRIB OR 36" x 44"
WALL- 40" x 54"
HANGING 45" X 60"

Mattress sizes:
CRIB: 27" x 52"
TWIN: 39" x 75"
DOUBLE: 54" x 75"
QUEEN: 60" x 80"
KING: 76" x 80"

QUILT = size of mattress PLUS number of inches you want the quilt to drop on both sides and bottom.

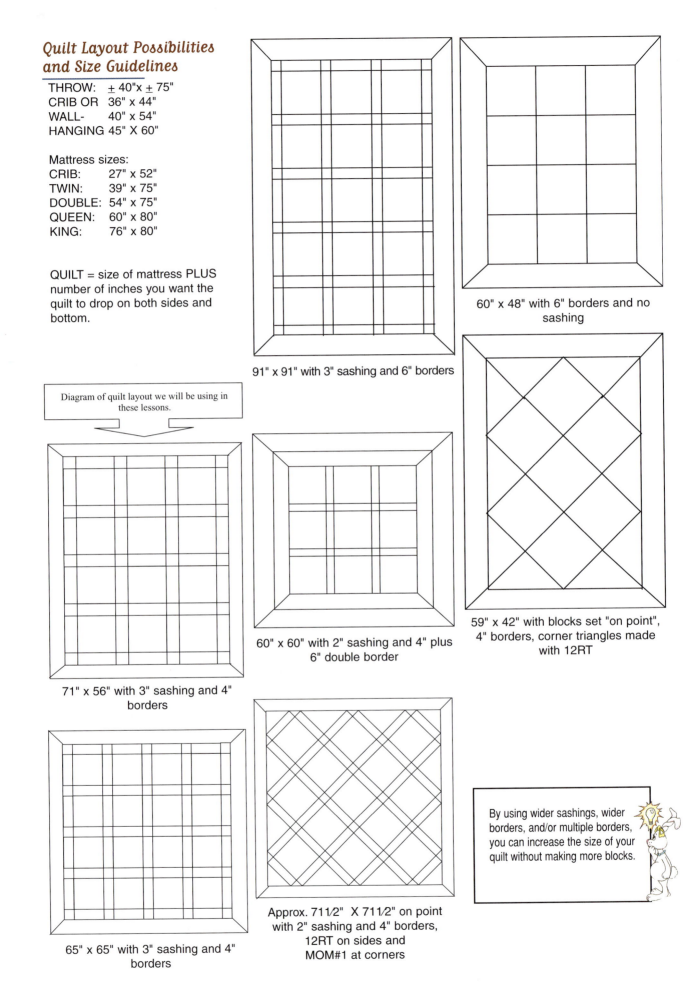

91" x 91" with 3" sashing and 6" borders

60" x 48" with 6" borders and no sashing

Diagram of quilt layout we will be using in these lessons.

71" x 56" with 3" sashing and 4" borders

60" x 60" with 2" sashing and 4" plus 6" double border

59" x 42" with blocks set "on point", 4" borders, corner triangles made with 12RT

65" x 65" with 3" sashing and 4" borders

Approx. 71½" X 71½" on point with 2" sashing and 4" borders, 12RT on sides and MOM#1 at corners

By using wider sashings, wider borders, and/or multiple borders, you can increase the size of your quilt without making more blocks.

Choosing Fabrics

One of my favorite sayings (and a truth I have learned the hard way) is, "Your work is only as good as your tools." I am especially referring to fabric. Some fabric manufacturers produce three grades of fabric. The fabric that is first run through the printing process is a loose-woven cotton or blend. This run-through is for adjusting the registration of the colors. You'll find the resulting fabrics are not wrapped on bolts but sold as flat-folds in discount department stores, etc. In the second run-through, the mill uses better quality cotton, but it is still fairly loose-woven, also. This production refines the printing process, and the resulting fabric is sold on bolts at chain fabric stores and discount stores. The last-run printing process uses the best, highest denier (more threads-per-inch) fabric. All the errors in printing have been corrected by this time. This bolt fabric goes to independent fabric shops and costs more, but you definitely get a higher-quality material.

I'm not recommending that you purchase your fabrics only from quilt shops. That wouldn't be reasonable. You should purchase the type of fabric appropriate to the quilt you will be making. When you give a quilt as a gift, you want the recipient to use your beautiful quilt, but you lose control of the care it will receive. Making a quilt requires an investment of many hours of work, and if you intend for it to be an heirloom that will be passed down in your family, I encourage you to purchase the best fabrics you can afford—and your first quilt may just become an heirloom.

When choosing your fabrics, always check the label on the end of the bolts to see where it is manufactured. If you see that the fabric is imported, assess how well it is made. Does the fabric have a nice feel *because it is closely woven, or because it is treated with sizing* (a finish that is applied to the surface of fabric to make it look and feel "crisp," but which will wash out)? Scrunch up a corner in the palm of your hand. If the wrinkles remain, it probably contains a lot of sizing. Be aware that fabric of lesser quality is more difficult to work with.

Fabric Colors and Patterns

Fabric manufacturers are closely tied to the fashion industry, and you'll find that colors and patterns go in and out of vogue frequently. That beautiful, vivid spring-green fabric that you just love may not be available next year when you really need it for a future quilt. If you see a fabric you love, buy it (at least 1/2 yard), because it may not be seen again for years. And after all, there *are* worse bad habits you can acquire besides fabric addiction!

Today, we are fortunate that there are so many beautiful, one hundred percent cotton fabrics from which to choose. They come in a myriad of color and design. Some patterned fabrics are made in more that one color combination—called a "colorway." Also, fabric manufacturers produce groupings of fabrics with colors and patterns made to go together. This helps us in coordinating our quilt fabrics.

When I work with beginning quilters, I find many are intimidated by the two most creative and effective components of a quilt: fabric designs and color choices. They feel unsure when they begin selecting specific fabrics for their quilts. Choosing the colors and patterns of fabrics can be the most enjoyable and exciting part of making your quilt. Actually, we all live with color, texture and pattern every day, and I can assure you that you know more than you think you do about them. You can successfully combine almost all fabrics as long as you understand and employ the principles of color value and pattern value as they relate to fabric choices.

Keep in mind that you will be spending many exacting hours sewing small patches of fabrics together to make an overall design. To make that design or block well defined and pleasing to look at, you will want to choose fabrics in colors that contrast. Select light-, medium-, and dark-colored fabrics—this is color value. If you used fabrics that were all one value (for example, all medium hues), from any distance you would not be able to distinguish one shape from another. Imagine that a block has a medium background. In order to make the patchwork design within the block visible, you would want to use light and/or dark fabrics to contrast against the medium background. This same principal holds true for light as well as dark backgrounds. **Contrast** is the key to making your patchwork designs distinct and recognizable.

Choose fabrics for pattern value by including **larger**, **medium**, and **smaller** prints. Many of the patches we will be cutting are small, so it is unwise to choose fabric that is patterned in a very large-scale print with spread-out colors. The smaller patches you cut will not contain all the colors you chose the fabric for and might not blend well within a block.

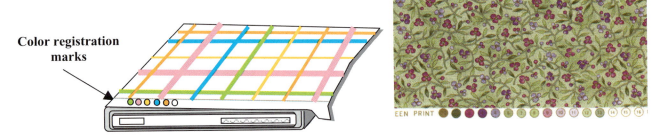

Color registration marks

EEN PRINT

The easiest way I know to choose fabrics for your quilt is to walk through the fabric shop and select your inspiration fabric first. This fabric will be one that you just "fall in love with" and will become the touchstone for colors in your quilt. Choose colors for the other fabrics that will coordinate with that inspiration piece. You can use the color registration marks on the margin or selvage edge of the fabric you have chosen to help you select complementary fabrics for your quilt. What are color registration marks? They are the little circles of colors in the selvage margin of fabric yardage. The little circles show all the colors contained in that fabric. When the fabric is printed, the dots of colors must fall within the circle outline to ensure the printing will be aligned.

Try to choose fabrics that enhance each other. They don't necessarily have to exactly match the colors in your inspiration fabric; you already have those shades. Choose fabrics that are darker and lighter in color value, and contain a variety of print patterns.

Gather your fabrics together so you can see the development of your fabric palette. Stack and "fan" them exposing a proportionate amount of each that you expect to use in your blocks. If you are undecided about a fabric choice, place it with your other fabrics, and then take it away. Ask yourself, "do I miss it?" If your answer is "yes," put it back. If you don't miss it, you probably like it for reasons other than how well it goes with your developing palette.

Over the next few lessons, you can continue to add fabrics to your collection, but by the time you have made the first third of your quilt blocks, you should have introduced all the fabrics you will use. This doesn't mean that you can't substitute one very similar fabric for another. In fact, done carefully, this adds interest to your blocks, but these "like-substitute" fabrics must have scale and coloration that is interchangeable.

The following is a list of fabric identifiers that will help you in adding variety to your fabric palettes:

Inspiration or theme fabrics—choose a fabric that beckons you to own it.

Stripes, geometric, graphic—these provide motion and carry direction, bringing the eye in or out.

Lights, mediums, darks—use your inspiration fabric to pick complementary fabrics; watch the scale of prints you choose, and include some (not too) large, medium and small prints.

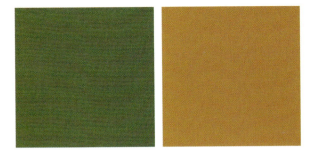

Solids—use with care they can say a lot and weigh heavily in a quilt. Their uncluttered surface demands attention and cries for quilting and that's why I like to use solid substitutes.

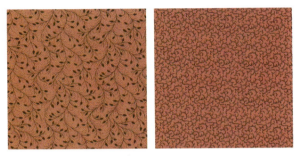

Solid substitutes or tone-on-tone—are printed fabrics with designs that are subtle and give the impression they are a solid color, but require much less quilting and lend support to a block.

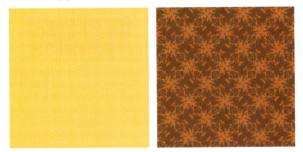

"Zinger"—usually a bright, attention-grabbing fabric (use sparingly).

Whimsical and pictorials—these give interest, pull the eye in.

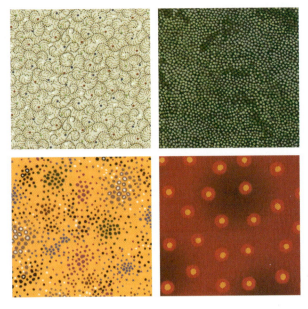

Dots, spots, and circles —these add fun, whimsy, interest; try to use one in every quilt.

Light givers—light, medium, and dark colors all in one fabric (plaids can be light givers).

How Many, How Much?

Some quilters are comfortable with more, but you need at least eight fabrics for variety and contrast. I'm from the "more is better" school, and have used over 30 in one sampler quilt. Seek *your* comfort zone.

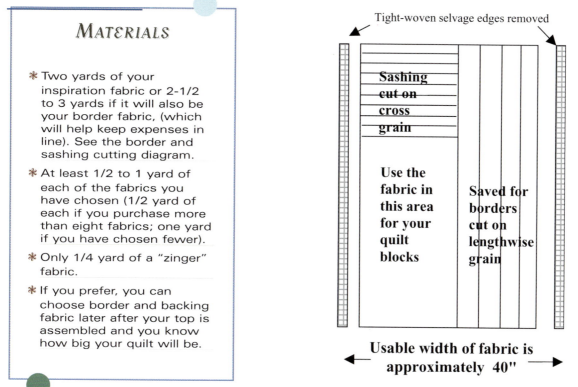

MATERIALS

* Two yards of your inspiration fabric or 2-1/2 to 3 yards if it will also be your border fabric, (which will help keep expenses in line). See the border and sashing cutting diagram.

* At least 1/2 to 1 yard of each of the fabrics you have chosen (1/2 yard of each if you purchase more than eight fabrics; one yard if you have chosen fewer).

* Only 1/4 yard of a "zinger" fabric.

* If you prefer, you can choose border and backing fabric later after your top is assembled and you know how big your quilt will be.

Tight-woven selvage edges removed

Sashing cut on cross grain

Use the fabric in this area for your quilt blocks

Saved for borders cut on lengthwise grain

Usable width of fabric is approximately 40"

Again, the more fabrics you purchase, the less you need of each, but 1/4 yard is the least amount you should buy, and this should be a "zinger" fabric, which every quilt needs—but not much of it!

Many years ago I made a Baltimore Album quilt. The colors I used were vibrant jewel tones. I did not pre-wash the fabrics. After the quilt top was completed, I sprayed it with water to remove the wash out marker I had used. Some of the fabrics bled onto the white background and it was impossible to remove all the stains.

Getting the Fabric Ready

I always rinse my fabrics after I bring them home from the store. Don't run them through a wash cycle, you'll loose a lot of fabric at the cut edges and it's not necessary. No matter how careful the mill is, some intensely colored fabrics will bleed. I wet my fabric down one piece at a time in an old, large, white porcelain dishpan where I can see if the colors run. If a fabric doesn't bleed, it gets wrung out and goes in the dryer with the other fabrics. If it does run, I rinse it over again once or twice until the rinse water is clear. If it still runs, I soak it in 1/4 cup white vinegar to a gallon of water then rinse again. If it still runs after that, I don't use it.

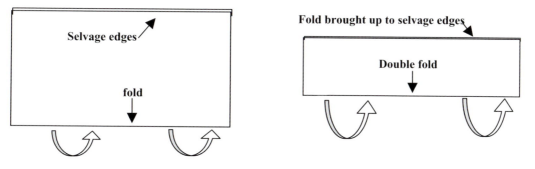

Selvage edges

fold

Fold brought up to selvage edges

Double fold

After the fabric is dry, square up the yardage and fold the piece in half meeting selvage edge to selvage edge so that the folded cloth hangs or lays wrinkle-free and straight. You may have to stretch the fabric on the bias to help it regain its "square." Spray with fabric sizing, and press it with an iron from selvage edge to the fold. Match the folded edge up to the two selvage edges, press again, and your fabric is ironed and folded in fourths ready to use. If you consistently do this, you can attack your stash and start working on a quilt in a moment's inspiration, confident that your fabric is pre-shrunk and ready to use.

Threads

You are not going to want to keep changing thread colors in your sewing machine to match fabrics as you piece your blocks, so I recommend that you purchase a neutral color thread that will blend with your fabrics. If your quilt will have mostly warm colors in it, try a taupe or beige. If the colors will be cool, try a gray. If you are using intense or very dark colors, you might want to use darker browns or grays. Of course, if your quilt fabrics are light in color, you can use white or off-white. See what looks the best. You don't want the thread to contrast with the fabrics you are using; you want it to blend in and disappear.

Needles

What size sewing machine needle? The most versatile size machine needle to use is 12/80. A 10/70 needle is also a good choice, but if you should accidentally hit a straight pin as you are sewing a seam, it will break more easily.

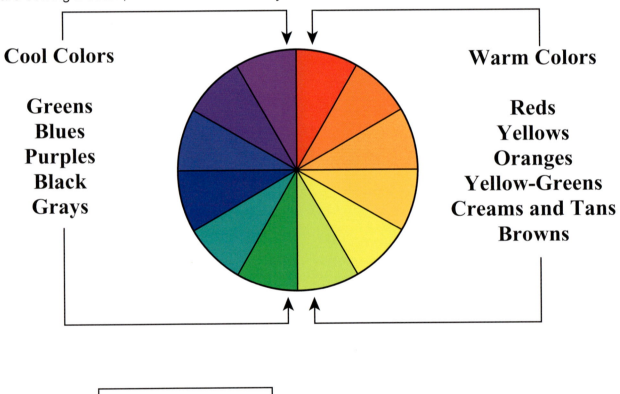

Cool Colors

Greens
Blues
Purples
Black
Grays

Warm Colors

Reds
Yellows
Oranges
Yellow-Greens
Creams and Tans
Browns

Remember to fill a couple of bobbins before you begin sewing. It seems you always run out of thread at the most inconvenient time.

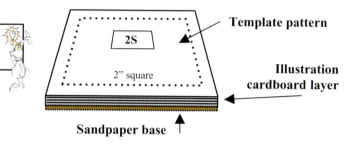

Read through this entire section on making templates before beginning this task.

Template pattern

2S

2" square

Illustration cardboard layer

Sandpaper base ↑

Practically Perfect Templates

In **The Essential Guide to Practically Perfect Patchwork**, templates are the patterns we use to cut most fabric patches. They consist of three layers: the paper pattern, illustration or cardboard in the middle, and a sandpaper base. Manufactured Plexiglas, plastic and metal templates are available for purchase; you are limited, however, to the specific blocks for which they were made. You can make your own templates, and you can make them to last your quilting lifetime. You only need to take your time and make them with care. When you have completed your templates, you will have durable tools that you can easily identify and use over and over again.

When cutting many identical patches, I have found it is easier to make a template for each shape and assembly-line cut from layers of folded fabric. This is not only easier, it is more accurate and less wasteful. Some quilters prefer to cut patches using only a rotary cutter and grid ruler, and we will employ this technique when making blocks such as the **Log Cabin**. But, we'll use a little trick to help line up the grid ruler to cut the correct size shapes every time.

You may wonder about the "different" identifiers used to label most of the templates. I don't know how many times I've looked through my personal collection for a group of templates I made from another source only to find most of them labeled "A", "B", "C", etc., and couldn't figure out which ones went together. Practically Perfect templates are labeled to reflect their type and **finished** measurements. Therefore, a square is identified as "S." A three-inch square is 3S. A two-inch by four-inch rectangle is labeled as 2X4R, and a two-inch by four-inch right triangle is labeled 2X4RT. Please remember that the **actual** measurements of all templates are 1/2" larger to reflect the addition of 1/4" seam allowances.

Be Accurate!

Your work will only be as good as your tools. Templates are tools. Patchwork is all about accuracy. All through these lessons you will be checking measurements, so start with accurate templates.

Making Durable Templates

At the end of Lessons 3 through 6, you will find paper template patterns to make into durable templates. They begin with the easiest shapes, squares, and advance to more complicated ones. To make your templates you will need:

MATERIALS
for making templates

* X-Acto or red-handled craft knife with a 24 blade or equivalent (a snap-off-type tool used for wallpaper allows the blade to wiggle and is not suitable for exact cutting)

* Paper scissors

* Medium weight cardboard or illustration board approximately 1/8" thick

* 5 sheets of medium or fine grade sandpaper

* Rubber cement with brush in the cap

* Rubber cement "Pick-Up" (optional) to clean up excess rubber cement

* Emery board

* Hard, textured surface like a cutting board or piece of Masonite at least 8" x 11" (Use the textured side of the Masonite)

* 12" or 18" metal ruler with cork backing

* .5 mm mechanical pencil with H or HB lead

* Template patterns from this book

Step 1: Separating the Paper Templates

As you begin Lessons 3 - 6, preserve each set of templates by making xerographic copies of them. **Be sure that the copies are exactly the same size as the originals**. Consistently use first copies, not a copy of a copy. With each lesson, cut the paper template copies apart from each other. **Do not cut on the bold lines; just separate the shapes from each other.** There are two 2S template patterns included so that you have one extra for practice. Making templates is just another skill you will acquire as you continue through these lessons.

Step 2: Rubber Cementing

Rubber cement is tricky stuff, but it is the only glue that won't wrinkle your paper template. (We're after accuracy here.) Additionally, if used as instructed, it will hold forever.

To create your first templates, lay your cut-out paper templates right side up on the illustration or cardboard. With a pencil, lightly draw around each piece. Leave about 1/4" between each template. You are designating a space on the cardboard where you will adhere the paper template. Remove your templates and flip them upside down onto scrap paper, getting them ready for cementing.

Brush rubber cement evenly and thinly on the backs of the template pieces. Then, brush rubber cement evenly and thinly onto the receiving areas you drew around them on the illustration board. Let both surfaces dry thoroughly. It will take a few minutes, depending upon how thickly you applied the rubber cement and how much humidity is in the air. Recap that rubber cement; it outgases and is flammable.

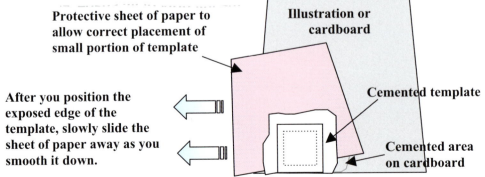

Protective sheet of paper to allow correct placement of small portion of template

After you position the exposed edge of the template, slowly slide the sheet of paper away as you smooth it down.

Illustration or cardboard

Cemented template

Cemented area on cardboard

Once two dried rubber-cemented surfaces touch each other, they will never come apart. To ensure proper placement of the paper template, place a clean sheet of any lightweight paper (typing/copy) over its cemented receiving spot on the cardboard. Expose a small area where you will adhere the first side of the template. Carefully align the template to the cemented receiving area you drew on the cardboard, and press to adhere. Slowly slide the clean sheet of paper away as you carefully smooth the rest of the template onto the cardboard. The back of the template and the cemented cardboard will adhere as soon as they touch each other. This sounds more complicated than it actually is, but it's the only safe way to avoid misplaced paper templates.

Continue to adhere all the pattern pieces to the illustration or cardboard in the same manner.

Take advantage of the straight edges of both the template and the cardboard. With scissors, cut the paper template on one straight line then adhere that edge to a straight cardboard edge. You can also use this trick for corners by cutting two 90 degree sides of the template and aligning them to a cardboard corner. Saves cutting with the craft knife!

Step 3: Cutting Out the Templates

Now, we have to cut the patterns apart so we can use them. For this we will need the red-handled craft knife and the metal ruler with the cork backing. (The cork backing prevents slipping.) Use a hard surface such as a cutting board or the wrong side of a piece of Masonite with its irregular non-slip surface. **Do not use a rotary cutting mat.**

Remember, a sharp blade is an accurate blade. A dull blade is a boo-boo waiting to happen.

NOTE: Only use a metal ruler with a cork backing when cutting out templates!

Be very careful how you place your fingers. Keep them well away from the action edge of the ruler.

Always place the ruler on top of the paper template. This keeps the knife blade at the outside edge of the bold cutting line and **protects the integrity of its shape.** Position the ruler **exactly on each line** you will cut. **Cut on the outside edge of the line.** Hold the craft knife securely, pressing the side of the blade against the ruler as a guide. Draw the **tip** of the blade down the ruler, slightly cutting into the cardboard. You don't have to use extreme pressure, and you don't have to cut all the way through with the first pass. Without moving the ruler, repeat the same cut, going deeper each time until you have cut through all layers of the cardboard. **Each pass will automatically cut deeper.** As you do cut deeper, the groove formed by the cut will help hold your blade in line. **Do not remove the ruler until you've made each cut all the way through the cardboard.** Repeat this process on all sides of the pattern piece until it is liberated from the rest of the cardboard. Follow this procedure for all pattern pieces. **When you are cutting narrowly-pointed pattern pieces, always cut toward the point.**

Step 4: Improved Non-skid Templates

You're almost done! We could use the templates you have made as they are now, but we can improve them so that they won't slide when we cut around them with our rotary cutters.

Take all your newly made templates and lay them right side up on the smooth side of a sheet of sandpaper. The sandpaper is going to become the bottom layer of our templates. Again, draw around each template onto the sandpaper. Repeat the cementing process. Lightly brush cement on the areas you just drew and on the bottoms of your template pieces. When both are dry, again use the clean paper sheet to carefully place the templates onto the receiving areas you drew for them on the sandpaper. This won't be as touchy as it was when you adhered the pattern pieces to the cardboard.

Carefully cut, freehanded (no ruler), around each template with the craft knife. Since you have been so careful in preparing the templates, you do not want the non-skid sandpaper base to be larger than your template. Therefore, **slant** the tip of the blade at an angle toward the template and **cut only the sandpaper.** This actually makes the sandpaper layer a little smaller than the template itself. Now you have a non-skid template!

Step 5: Finishing Touches

You can use an emery board to carefully smooth any rough edges. Also, there is a product called rubber cement "Pick-Up" found in art supply stores that will remove any excess rubber cement; simply rubbing off the excess with your fingers will accomplish the same task. Keep in mind, though, that dried rubber cement erases just like an eraser.

Homework

Make templates for Lesson 3—Squares, Rectangles, and Half-Square Triangles—which begins on the next page. You don't have to make a template for the 6" square if you don't want to. (I don't always make a cardboard template for minimum-use, larger patches. We will cut that patch with our rotary ruler and cutter.) Also have your fabric pre-shrunk, pressed, folded, and ready for the next lesson. We will be constructing:

- **Log Cabin** or **Courthouse Steps** block to identify accurate seam allowances.
- **Four-Patch** block to learn perfect intersections.
- A block containing half-square triangles to learn how to eliminate bias.
- Challenge: one other block of your choice just for fun.

Our lessons build on all the templates in this workbook. We will be using some of them in more than one lesson. By choosing which blocks you want to construct, you can limit how many templates you will have to make for each lesson. Instructions for each block show which templates are needed. Just make sure that you choose to make a block from each construction technique category.

Squares, Rectangles, and Half-Square Triangles
*L*ESSON 3

Find and Use Accurate Seam Allowances

Log Cabin Traditional Set
"Logs" are sewn in a clockwise fashion around the center square.

Courthouse Steps Set
"Logs" are attached to the center square: top, bottom, left, right.

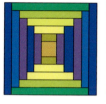

Make Perfect Intersections

Four-Patch
This humble little block is the foundation of many patchwork quilt block patterns.

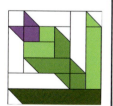

Half-Square Triangles – NO BIAS!
Bluebell
Another log cabin assembly similar to Thistle.

Thistle
This block is similar to a log cabin with larger "logs." It is assembled off-center.

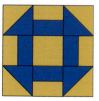

Hole in the Barn Door
You'll build confidence making this block – no diagonal intersections to match.

CHALLENGES

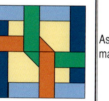

Snowball & Nine-Patch
Here you can practice joining diagonal seams to perpendicular seams.

Road to Oklahoma
A complete quilt top of this block makes an over-all directional pattern.

Loop the Loop
Assembled edge-to-edge Loop the Loop makes a wonderful "fool the eye" quilt.

Four Hearts
This block requires careful piecing. Be sure you use a *scant* 1/4" seam allowance!

A completed block will measure 12-1/2" X 12-1/2"; when it is sewn into the quilt top, its finished measurements will be 12" X 12".

Using the Rotary Cutter, Mat, and Ruler

In this lesson, we begin to cut the patches we'll sew into blocks that will be assembled into our quilt top. We'll start with squares, rectangles, and half-square triangles because they are the easiest shapes to work with. We will use the rotary cutter, mat, ruler, and templates instead of scissors because we can more quickly and accurately cut out many identical patches at the same time from pressed and folded fabric as shown in the first lesson.

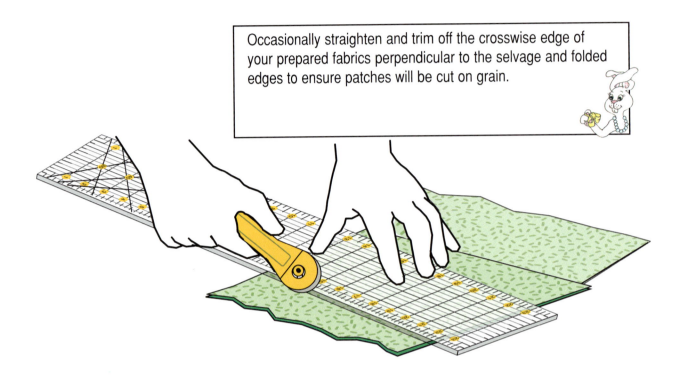

Occasionally straighten and trim off the crosswise edge of your prepared fabrics perpendicular to the selvage and folded edges to ensure patches will be cut on grain.

Rotary Cutter Safety

A dull rotary cutter is like a dull knife; both do the best job if they are sharp and can be the cause of damage if they are not. Unfortunately, as expensive as they are, rotary blades become dull with use fairly quickly, so watch for sales and have a supply on hand when you begin a project. Actually, you can purchase rotary blade sharpeners, but blades can be sharpened only a limited number of times.

When you were using the craft knife to cut your templates, you positioned bent fingers on top of the ruler well away from the ruler edge. This is the same position you must use when cutting with the rotary cutter. Expose the blade facing the ruler for cutting. Always cut away from yourself, and always retract the blade after each cut. Anchor your "ruler" hand by placing your ring and little fingers off the ruler on the fabric. When making a long cut, "crawl" your fingers up the ruler parallel to the rotary cutter; in other words, cut as far as across from your fingertips, crawl your "ruler" hand up the ruler (retaining pressure on the ruler and being careful not to move it) as many times as necessary to complete the cut.

Having an additional small cutting mat is so helpful for the detail work of rotary cutting patches. You can place your partially-cut fabric patch on the smaller mat and turn the mat instead of the fabric. The little mats are inexpensive, and having the flexibility to turn your work to a more accessible angle without disturbing the fabric ensures you won't cheat and cut across or toward yourself.

The Inherent Characteristics of Woven Fabrics

All fabrics are made with tightly-woven selvage edges on both long (lengthwise) sides; therefore, the lengthwise grain of fabric runs parallel to the selvage edges. The lengthwise grain does not stretch. The crosswise grain runs perpendicular to the selvage edges of fabric and "gives" a little. True bias is 45 degrees from either lengthwise or crosswise grain and stretches a great deal. By being aware of these fabric characteristics, we can use them to our advantage and limit the amount of difficulty their improper use can cause.

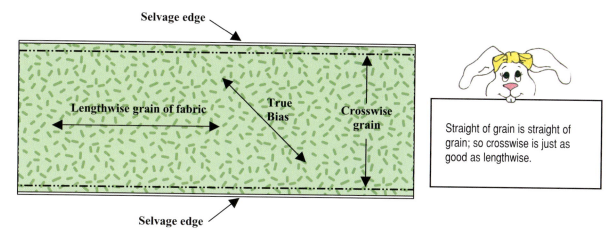

Straight of grain is straight of grain; so crosswise is just as good as lengthwise.

You will notice that each template pattern included in this book has an arrow on it that indicates straight of grain (crosswise or lengthwise). When placing and cutting your patches, pay attention to the grainline arrows marked on each template. Orient each template squarely on the straight of either grain. Although you might be tempted to use the selvage edge of your fabric because you can be certain your patches will be cut on the straight of grain, you will regret using it because its extra-tight weave will act differently from the rest of the material in the patch and cause problems. Use the selvage edge only as a *reference* of grainline.

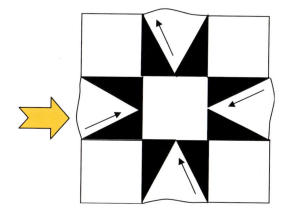

Also, be mindful to control where the bias sides of patches will appear. This means that as we construct our patchwork blocks, the lengthwise or crosswise grain should be at the outside edges of the assembled units as well as the completed block; *no* bias on any outside edges, unless you want ruffles.

A Little Patchwork Terminology

In this instruction, **patches** are the individually shaped pieces we will cut and assemble into **sub-units**. Sub-units will be assembled into larger groupings called **units**. Units will be assembled into **blocks**.

How to Cut Patches

Begin with a straight new cut **on the crosswise grain** (perpendicular to the folded and selvage edges) of your prepared fabric pieces.

Be careful when cutting patches; you don't want to cut into your cardboard templates. Take your time. Don't "attack" the fabric. Use the template edges as barriers to guide the rotary cutter as you cut. Treat your templates as tools that you must use carefully so they will retain their accuracy.

• Using the **Four-Patch** block as an example, you can see from the color diagram on the first page of this lesson that it is made of 16 squares using only four colors of fabric. You'll need four squares of two colors; six squares of one color; and two squares of a fourth color.

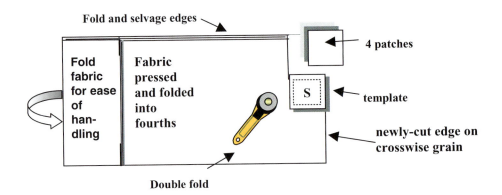

• After you have cut one set of patches, you can use the remaining cut edge as the first cut line for another set of patches.

• Open your folded fabrics if you need less than four patches. You can layer your fabrics and cut two or more different colors at the same time.

• When cutting, hold the template firmly, keeping your fingers away from the edges. Cut away from yourself. *Gently pull excess fabric away from that which is under the template.* You can see if your cut is complete without disturbing the patch. If the fabric is not cut all the way through, you can re-cut. Use more downward pressure with the next cut.

• After making a cut, *always* close the blade.

- You don't have to use templates if you're only going to cut one or two patches like the 6" square for **Snowball and Nine-Patch**, or if the block you will be making consists of strips easily measured and cut using the rotary ruler, as in the **Log Cabin** and **Courthouse Steps** blocks. See the individual instructions for these blocks.

Patchwork's Golden Measure

We will use a straight machine stitch to sew our patches together, but before you begin to sew, it is important to understand the necessity for accuracy in seam allowances. **The patterns in this book use a scant 1/4" seam allowance. The completed blocks measure 12-1/2" by 12-1/2" before assembly into the quilt.** You can imagine if you make only 1/16th of an inch error on each seam multiplied by eight seams, for example, your completed block will be 1/2" off in size. (Don't fear, though, if your blocks are slightly off, there is a fix-up remedy that will be presented in Lesson 7.) Do try your best to sew consistent, scant 1/4" seam allowances.

Where is the Scant Quarter-Inch Mark on the Machine?

There isn't one! But, we can find it. You can buy a special foot for most machines whose left edge is a scant 1/4" from the needle. You would use that left edge as a guide to make a scant 1/4" seam. If you don't have a special foot, you can find the scant quarter-inch mark on your sewing machine by using your rotary ruler. Since you will be using your rotary ruler during the quilt-making process, always use it as your uniform measuring tool. If you purchase other rulers later because you need a different shape or size, buy the same brand to avoid discrepancies from one manufacturer to another.

Place the ruler under the presser foot and drop the foot down to hold the ruler, positioning

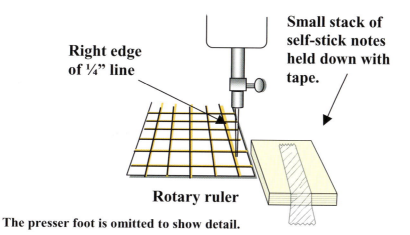

Right edge of ¼" line

Small stack of self-stick notes held down with tape.

Rotary ruler

The presser foot is omitted to show detail.

the needle hole under the 1/4" line at the right edge. Slowly rotate the flywheel to move the needle down to touch the right side of the 1/4" line. A small stack (four to six) of little self-stick notes taped alongside the edge of the ruler and in front of the foot helps you line up your patches, and guides them straight toward the needle. You can also purchase self-stick guides or use a strip of moleskin. Observe where the scant 1/4" mark is in relation to the edge of your machine's foot or feed dogs, and make a mental note.

Stitch a sample 1/4" seam joining two 2" square scraps of fabric. Press the patches open. Check the measurement across the middle of the patches. It should be 4-1/2". If it isn't, make adjustments using the same procedure.

Next Step — Pinning

Select the first two pieces that will be sewn to each other, overlay them right sides together matching raw edges on the side to be sewn, and pin them together with the pin slightly away from the outer edge. Don't take too big a "bite" as it distorts the edges when sewing. Don't sew over pins. You will break your needles and bend your pins. Sewing over pins also distorts the seam line.

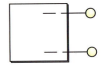

Correct pin placement

> OK, I confess. I do sew over pins occasionally. I'm very careful to do it slowly. Sometimes a point just needs to be held while you sew over it. Also, I don't keep my straight pins corralled on a magnet anymore. My friend, Debbie, told me it magnetizes the pins, and when you sew over them, they're sure to attract the needle and break it! She's right!

Take Me to Your Leader

What's a scrap leader? It's a piece of scrap fabric you use when beginning to sew your fabric patches together. Start sewing with a doubled-over scrap of fabric, and then feed your layered patches into the needle. The scrap at the beginning prevents the needle from punching the leading edge of the upcoming fabric patches into the needle hole. Plus it gives you something to hold on to when keeping the threads taut as you begin a line of stitching.

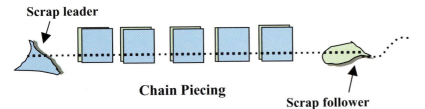

Scrap leader

Chain Piecing

Scrap follower

Chain Piecing

Chain piecing is a streamlined technique that enables you to sew many two-patch sub-units together very quickly. Simply pin a number of two patches together, then sew assembly line fashion almost butting each successive sub-unit one after another. Leave a few stitches of thread between each sub-unit and sew a "scrap follower" at the end of your chain. Clip off the patches leaving the "scrap follower" to become the next "leader."

Pressing Your Patchwork: Seam Allowances — Step to One Side!

I know you think you're learning how to sew patches, but in truth, you'll be using your iron almost as much as you use your sewing machine in patchwork construction. Did you know there's a difference between ironing and pressing? Ironing is what you do to clothing. Pressing is how you "iron" patchwork.

After sewing two patches together, press the seam line as sewn to "set in" the stitches and make it easier to press the patches apart. **In almost all applications, seam allowances will be pressed to one side with the right side of the fabric facing up as you press. This strengthens seams.** Seam allowances are not pressed "open." If seam allowances would be pressed open, the only thing that would hold patches together would be the thread that joined them. By pressing seams to one side, other seams that cross the seam allowances will strengthen the join.

Do not slide the iron back and forth over your assembled seams. This will stretch and distort your work. Press your patchwork with a kind of up-and-down motion. Use **no steam** as it also stretches fabric and burns fingers. When you complete each block, you can spray it with

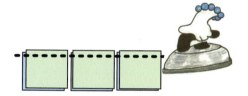

Pressing and "setting in" a line of stitching

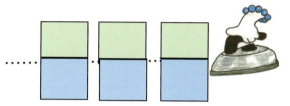

Pressing sub-units open with seam allowance to darker fabric, if possible

fabric sizing, square it up, and give it a good overall press.

Floating Seam Allowance

If you have a choice, you will want to position the joined patches so that the seam allowances will be pressed to the darker fabric to keep them from shadowing through the lighter patches on the quilt top. Sometimes you will need to press one seam allowance in two different directions to press to the dark fabric. This is called a floating seam allowance.

Although pressing to the darker fabric is the ideal, my practical advice is to press seam allowances for ease of construction. If a sliver of darker fabric shadows through to the top under a lighter fabric, trim away the offending darker fabric.

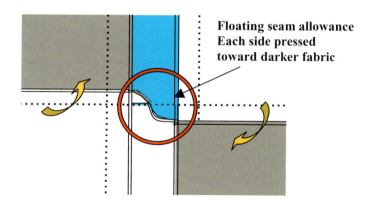

Floating seam allowance Each side pressed toward darker fabric

The key to making intersections meet perfectly is opposing seam allowances. To accomplish this, use the press to nest principal. This one technique and its applications will give you the power to control how easy it is to construct your patchwork blocks.

You will be sewing many pieced units together with other like units; when joined, you will want the resulting points at seam intersections to meet perfectly, not overlap or not quite touch each other. To accomplish this "miraculous feat," simply place two pieced units that are to be joined, right sides together. Since you have already pressed the seam allowances to one side, just make sure the sides will end up in opposition; in other words, both units will have their seam allowances pressed to the right, but when you stack them right sides together, the seam allowances will be facing in opposite directions. This is called nesting. Feel for a tight nesting fit at the seam, and place pins into the seam allowances on both sides of the seams through all layers as shown. Sew the joining seam, removing each pin after the sewing machine needle is **within each seam allowance**, but just before the needle reaches the pin. Removing the pin after the machine needle is within the seam allowance will prevent any shifting.

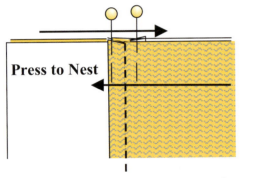

Press to Nest

Opposing seam allowances pressed and
pinned to "nest"

=

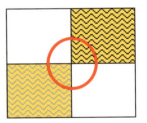

**No overlap; all four corners
meet—practically perfectly!**

Creative Pressing

When you press your seams to one side, it may make a difference how "perfect" they look depending upon which direction the seam allowance is pressed. After sewing, you can press those seam allowances to make YOU look good! Don't forget to trim any allowance that shadows through to the front.

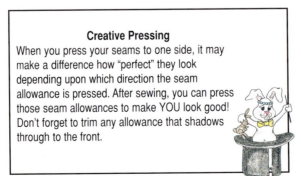

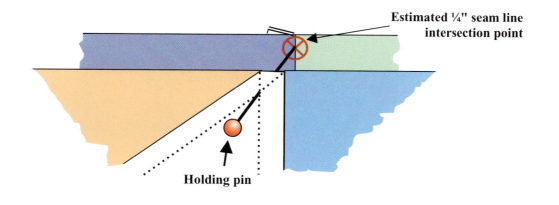

Estimated ¼" seam line
intersection point

Holding pin

The Holding Pin

Matching other configurations such as diagonal and/or straight seams at intersections presents a real challenge. Let's use the example of joining a unit consisting of two squares to another sub-unit of one square and half-square triangles.

In the illustration, two joined squares are face-up behind the square/half-square triangle unit. First, anticipate in which direction you will need the "square/half-square triangle unit" seam allowance pressed so that you can see the triangle intersection you will be matching. Then press the seam allowances of the "squares" sub-unit in opposition. With right sides together, insert a holding pin in the apex of the angle of the top sub-unit. Estimate where the 1/4" seam line will fall on the "squares" sub-unit. Continue to insert that same pin in the anticipated 1/4" seam line on the second sub-unit. Nest seam allowances in the same way we did for squares and rectangles, and pin. Sew 1/4" seam **one thread** above apex (closer to the cut edge) to provide "turning space."

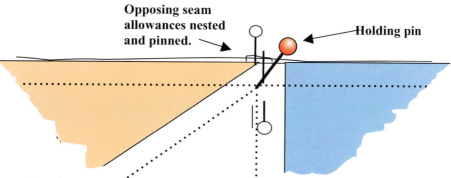

Opposing seam
allowances nested
and pinned.

Holding pin

Holding pin shown in correct position. Note seam line is sewn one thread above intersecting seams. Remove holding pin after machine needle is into seam allowance just before needle would hit it.

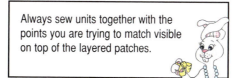

Always sew units together with the points you are trying to match visible on top of the layered patches.

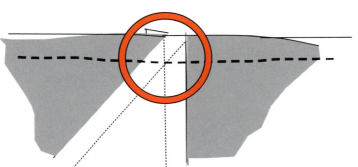

More than ¼" to raw edge at apex of join—seam allowance gets gradually wider to cross one thread above target point, then returns to ¼".

If you encounter a sub-unit with a target intersection point that is slightly more or less than 1/4" from the raw edge, gauge your distance and *gradually* decrease or increase the seam allowance to within one thread of the apex, then *gradually* return to 1/4" as you finish the seam. Stop and remove holding pin after your needle is **into** the seam allowance and just before you will cross at apex.

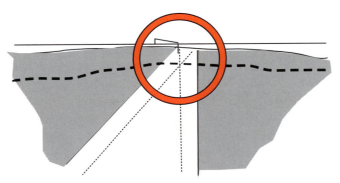

Not quite ¼" to raw edge at apex of join—seam allowance gets gradually narrower and crosses one thread above target point, then returns to ¼".

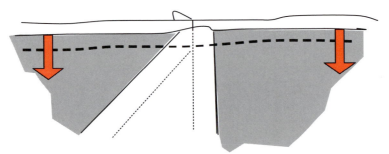

Drop smaller unit down and sew standard ¼" seam

If both units are just slightly smaller than needed, you can adjust the seam allowance where necessary by sewing a seam narrower than 1/4". If only one unit is small, just drop that unit down slightly and pretend it's the right size, then sew your 1/4" seam. Check to ensure there is enough fabric in the seam allowance (at least 1/8") to keep the units from pulling apart. Fear not if you can't make any correction at this time. As long as your blocks are sewn securely together, there are a few tricks we will learn later to alter the size of the finished blocks.

Making Half-Square Triangles

In Lesson 4, you will learn how to deal with triangle patches and their natural inclination to stretch out of shape. For this lesson, though, we will use the "half-square triangle" method to make triangle patches. I always use this technique whenever I need to make small triangles. It is a little wasteful, but very accurate, and you can use your leftovers for "scrap leaders."

Light square on top

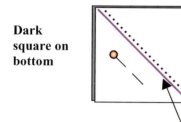

Dark square on bottom

Draw and sew

To make half-square triangles, start with two square patches of the same size. Layer the squares with right sides together. Using your ruler and a .5mm mechanical pencil, draw a diagonal line through the center of the top square. Even though you draw the line diagonally from corner to corner, usually one triangle side of the line will be a little larger than the other (possibly caused by the distortion created by drawing on fabric instead of paper). The larger side is the side you will keep. To help you remember, pin the patches together in the larger side.

Sew the two patches together on the right edge of the drawn line, **favoring the side you will be using.** This gives the seam "turning space." Cut off the excess triangle shape, leaving 1/4" seam allowance.

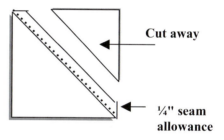

Cut away

¼" seam allowance

Wrong Side   **Right side**

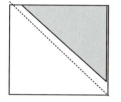 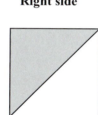

Press seam allowance to dark patch

This is how the half square triangle sub-unit should look.

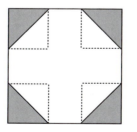

Smaller squares placed over corners of larger square and sewn on diagonal.

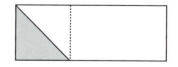

Square placed over rectangle, sewn together on diagonal of square.

The half-square triangle technique can be used with a square + rectangle, and a small square + large square. The most important thing to remember in using this technique is to look at the block pattern and determine which way the diagonal line should go when drawn on the wrong side of one square, so that it will be oriented correctly on the right side of the sub-unit. Just like carpenters do, check it twice, cut it once.

Ready, Set, Sew

When sewing patches together, it is not desirable to backstitch at the beginning and end of each seam, as you would do in garment construction. The "backward" stitches hardly ever go into the same line of stitching, so the width of the seam allowance could be affected. Instead, choose a shorter stitch length that is about 12 stitches to an inch. Because patches are so small, I hardly ever take out stitches. Most of the time I'll just re-cut the patches and start over. As you are assembling your blocks, you will eventually come to a point where you'll have to take out stitches or cut and sew more units and sub-units, and 12 per inch isn't too difficult to remove.

In Lesson 5 we will backstitch at the beginning and ending of seams that undergo stress as they are sewn. But, as my Mom used to say, we don't have to buy that ticket until we board the train.

The Patterns and Instructions

All of the block patterns presented in this workbook appear twice, once grouped in color at the beginning of each lesson so you can see how the patches that make them up are used, and once as a line drawing next to the specific directions for making the blocks. It will be very helpful to you if you color in the line drawings with crayons, colored pencils or markers approximating your fabric colors to aid you in assembling your patches. Keep your diagram in front of you as you stitch your blocks together.

Each pattern gives a little information about the block, indicates which templates to use and some list how many patches you will need to cut. Additional assembly instructions, tips, and techniques are shown as you will need them.

Homework

The patterns and templates for Lesson 3, Squares, Rectangles and Half-Square Triangles, follow. Now, for your assignment, should you choose to accept it:

- Make either the **Log Cabin** traditional set or **Courthouse Steps** blocks. Remember the importance of accurate scant 1/4" seam allowances … any discrepancy will show here. Read the instructions beside the black and white line drawing. Watch for the "magic trick" you can perform as you attach the last two logs.
- Make the **Four-Patch** block. It will give you the practice you need to make "perfect" intersecting seams.
- Choose and make a half-square triangle block. Here is where you'll master the diagonal/straight seam intersection. Use the "holding pin" technique for combination seam intersection construction.
- Optional: Choose and make any other block from the Challenges.
- Make templates for Lesson 4, Triangles.

If one of your fabrics tends to stretch, sew with the "difficult" fabric placed against the feed dogs. Pin the beginning and ending edges squarely and let the feed dogs do the work of easing in excess fullness. You will be surprised how this little trick will automatically take care of any unruly fabric patches. This method also works when sewing two units together if one is slightly larger than the other.

You'll soon be wondering why I had you go to all the trouble of making durable templates when you see the first two patterns. Both **Log Cabin** and **Courthouse Steps** could be made using templates, but why bother making them when it's so much easier to cut strips with your rotary cutter? Don't worry! There are plenty of opportunities coming up to use templates. I just wanted to make you aware of other options. As mentioned, plastic templates are commercially available for some of the shapes I've given you in this book. But, you're limited to specific sizes, and it becomes quite expensive to purchase all the template shapes you can make from this book, if you can find them.

Just as the pioneers first cut down many trees for logs to build their cabins, we're going to pre-cut an assortment of fabric "logs" with our rotary tools before we construct our blocks. Having our fabrics pressed and folded in fourths is going to make this preparation work easy.

When using the grid rotary ruler to cut patches, it's helpful to place a few small self-stick notes on the under side of the ruler along the grid line you will be referencing. Position the sticky edge right on the line, having the rest of the note extend away from that line. Then, when you align your ruler against the raw edge of a fabric to cut each "log," the note will act as a flag so you won't line up to the wrong measurement. It will also act as a "stop" so that the ruler won't slide.

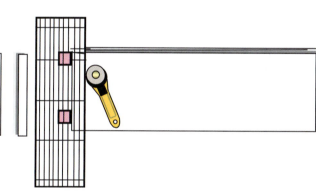

You may want to remember and use this technique whenever you need a number of shapes easily cut with rotary tools, including squares, rectangles, and triangles of various sizes that are quite large; i.e., the 12-1/2" square or triangle you will need in upcoming lessons.

Strip width for the Log Cabin-type blocks finishes 1", which means we have to cut them 1-1/2" to include two 1/4" seam allowances. Strip lengths are given in the pattern and include seam allowances. Don't be tempted to sew a strip onto the growing center square and then cut it off using the already-sewn patches as a gauge. That's not an accurate way to measure length because there's the possibility that the narrow strips will stretch.

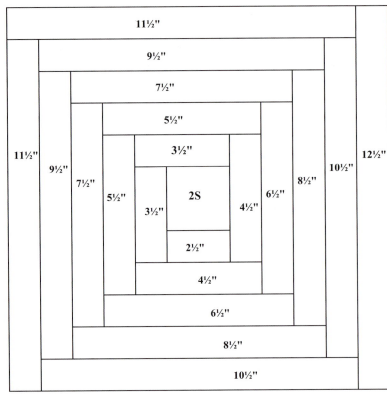

Templates: 2S
There are no other templates.

About this block: Log Cabin is a basic block that will teach the importance of accurate seam allowances. The contrast of light and dark plays an important role when it is made into a whole quilt. Depending upon how you arrange them, numerous secondary designs, known by such names as **Barn Raising**, **Straight Furrows**, etc., can be created. Here, the dark fabrics are on the top and right side, and the light fabrics are on the bottom and left side. In traditional blocks, the center square (2S) was either red to denote "fire in the hearth" or yellow to denote "light in the window" of the log cabin. Color this line drawing to approximate your fabrics repeating colors (fabrics) as needed.

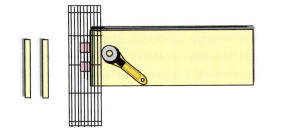

Step 1: Using the grid ruler, cut strips that are 1-1/2" wide from the folded and pressed fabrics you prepared. The number of strips you cut will be determined by how many fabrics you will use. Fabric "logs" can be repeated. Just keep darks with darks and lights with lights. Start with one long strip of each light and dark fabric. Unfolded, those strips will be 1-1/2" by approximately 40". Remember, you don't want to use the selvage edge in a patch.

Step 2: Cut one **each** light and dark "logs" that are **1-1/2" wide** by **3-1/2", 4-1/2", 5-1/2", 6-1/2", 7-1/2", 8-1/2" 9-1/2", and 10-1/2"**. Cut one light log that is **2-1/2"** long and another that is **11-1/2"** long. Don't cut the last **11-1/2"** and **12-1/2"** dark logs until you have assembled the rest of the block. All these measurements include the 1/4" seam allowance.

Step 3: With a scant 1/4" seam allowance, begin sewing the center 2S patch to the 2-1/2" light log. Continue to attach logs as shown in the diagram alternating light, dark, dark, light, etc., around the center square in clockwise fashion. Make previously attached logs fit the new ones by placing the larger log against the feed dogs and easing in fullness. As you add each log, press seam allowances away from the center.

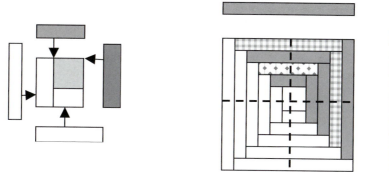

Step 4: Before you attach the last two "logs," press your block well and measure across the **middle** of your almost-completed block from:

side to the side   = _____inches   and   top to the bottom = _____inches

Your almost-finished **Log Cabin** block should measure 11-1/2" X 11-1/2". If it doesn't, the last two logs may need to be cut **wider** than 1-1/2". (Don't worry, when assembled into your quilt top, no one will be able to tell they are wider.) With this adjustment, you can be certain your finished block will be 12-1/2" X 12-1/2".

Subtract your **side-to-side** measurement from the goal of 12-1/2". Do the same for the **top to bottom** measurement. Add 1/2" for seam allowances to each remainder, and you will get the exact width you will need to cut each of the last two logs.

Insert your measurements:

	12-1/2"ideal side		12-1/2" ideal top to bottom
	-____" Actual		-____" actual
	difference		difference
	+ 1/2"seam allowance		+ 1/2"seam allowance
New width of	____" last side log		____" last top log

Step 5: If necessary, cut and attach the last two dark logs using your calculated new width measurement. The lengths of the logs should still be 11-1/2" and 12-1/2". **OR....**

If your almost-finished block is larger than 11-1/2" X 11-1/2", go ahead and cut the last two logs 1-1/2" by 11-1/2" and 12-1/2", respectively, then attach as before. Your block will be larger than 12-1/2" square and will be trimmed to size later when we assemble the top. Since your block is larger, go back and correct the seam allowance reference line you marked on your machine.

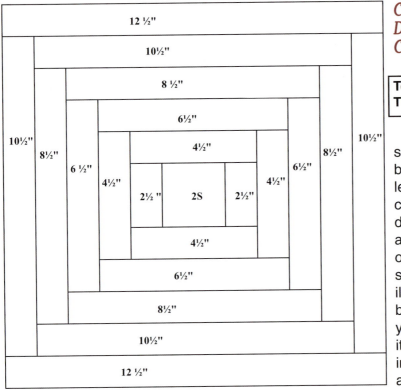

Templates: 2S
There are no other templates.

About this block: As you can see from the color illustration of blocks at the beginning of this lesson, **Courthouse Steps** has coloration that is also light versus dark, but here the lights and darks are opposite each other with light on top and bottom and dark on the sides. This creates the optical illusion of depth. Because this block, too, has so many seams, you probably guessed that making it will impress you with the importance of accurate seam allowances.

Step 1: Prepare and cut 1-1/2" fabric strips as for traditional **Log Cabin**.

Step 2: Cut two **each** light and dark logs that are **1-1/2" wide** by **4-1/2", 6-1/2", 8-1/2"**. Cut one dark log **1-1/2" wide** by **10-1/2"** long. Cut two dark logs that are **1-1/2" wide** by **2-1/2"** long. Cut one light log **1-1/2" wide** by **12-1/2"** long and two that are **10-1/2"** long.

Step 3: Instead of attaching logs clockwise to the center 2S patch, these logs are sewn first side-to-side then top and bottom, repeating until after you attach the third 10-1/2" log.

Step 4: Follow the instructions detailed in the **Log Cabin Traditional Set** directions for measuring and cutting the width of the last 10-1/2" log and the last 12-1/2" log. Unfortunately, you will have to make your calculations twice: Once when you measure to add the last 10-1/2" log, then again when you add the last 12-1/2" log.

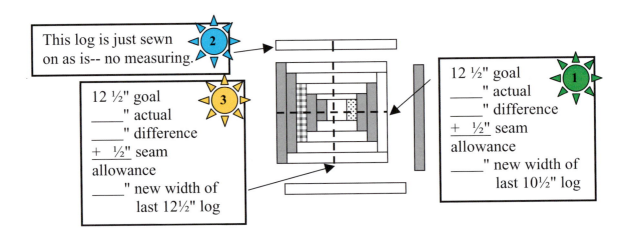

1	2		
3	4		

Simple Four-Patch Block

Templates: 3S = Cut 16 patches

About this block: The **Four-Patch** is one of the most basic traditional blocks. It is believed to be the first block taught to a young girl just learning to piece patchwork. The form of this block is used as a foundation for much more intricate block combinations, which you will see as you progress through this book. Color in this diagram to help you decide fabric placement. By sewing this block, you will learn how to make perfect intersections.

Step 1: Join eight sets of two squares together **according to your colored diagram** to get eight rectangle units. Assembling this block presents an excellent opportunity to practice chain piecing as shown in this lesson.

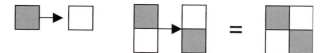

Step 2: Following your color guide, sew two rectangle sub-units together to get a four-patch square. Press to nest to create perfect intersections. Create floating seam allowances or press for ease of construction. If necessary, use "imaginative seam allowances." Repeat this process three more times to make (four) four-patch units. You've almost completed this block!

Step 3: In the same way you joined the rectangle sub-units into a square, nest and pin, then sew two sets of four squares together. You now have two halves of the block that measure approximately 12-1/2" X 6-1/2".

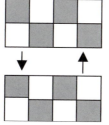

Step 4: Join the two halves together pressing to nest, and you are finished. Congratulations!

It is more accurate to assemble patchwork (or even whole quilts) in block segments as we did units 1, 2, 3, and 4. If assembled in rows, the seams will take on a wavy look.

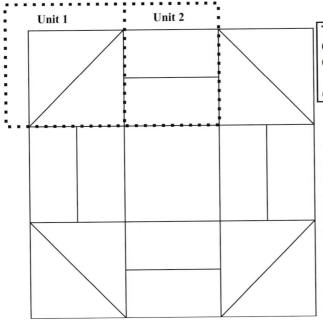

| Templates: 4S = |
| Cut 4 of one color |
| Cut 5 of second color |
| 2X4R = |
| Cut four of each color |

About this block: Hole in the Barn Door is also known as Churn Dash. It is a nine-patch, which is another basic, traditional block. Choose two colors that contrast well for your patches. By stitching this block, you will be practicing the half-square triangle technique.

Step 1: Refer to half-square triangle instructions and make four half-square triangles. Press seam allowances to darker fabric. This is Unit 1.

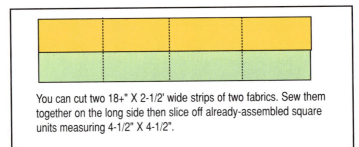

You can cut two 18+" X 2-1/2' wide strips of two fabrics. Sew them together on the long side then slice off already-assembled square units measuring 4-1/2" X 4-1/2".

Step 2: To make Unit 2 you can cut and join two different color rectangles on the long sides, or you can follow the short cut above. Make four like units. Press seam allowances to darker fabric.

Step 3: Assemble the first and third rows of this block by joining two of Unit 1 to opposite sides of Unit 2. Press seam allowances to the darker fabric.

Step 4: Assemble the middle row by rotating the remaining Units 2 and attaching to opposite sides of 4S. Put your press to nest method to work here. If you have pressed the seam allowances in rows 1 and 3 **away from** the center unit, press the seam allowances in row 2 **towards** the center square, or vice versa.

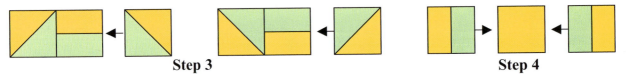

Step 3   **Step 4**

Step 5: Join rows 1and 3 to row 2, nesting seams. "Creative Press" the long seam allowances to whichever sides give the face of the block the most accurate look.

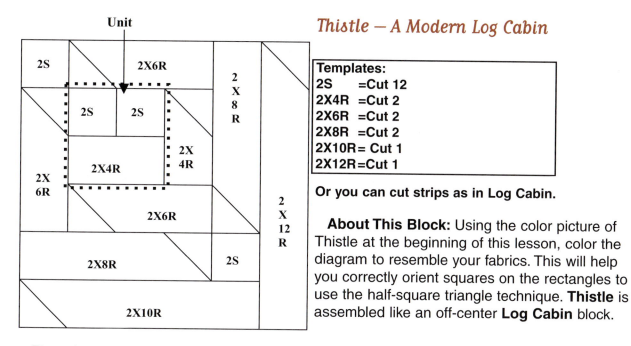

Templates:

2S	=Cut 12
2X4R	=Cut 2
2X6R	=Cut 2
2X8R	=Cut 2
2X10R	= Cut 1
2X12R	=Cut 1

Or you can cut strips as in Log Cabin.

About This Block: Using the color picture of Thistle at the beginning of this lesson, color the diagram to resemble your fabrics. This will help you correctly orient squares on the rectangles to use the half-square triangle technique. **Thistle** is assembled like an off-center **Log Cabin** block.

There is one whole 2X4R patch and four whole 2S patches in this block. There are eight 2S patches that are used to make half-square triangles at the ends of the rectangles. Do you see why it is so helpful to be able to refer to a color diagram as you cut out the patches to make **Thistle**? It's a challenge, but I know you can do it. As you cut your patches, arrange them into the **Thistle** block laying the 2S patches on top of the rectangles you will be joining to them.

Step 1: Join two of the **2S** patches that make part of the **Thistle** flower and add 2X4R to make Unit 1.

As you make Thistle, press the seam allowances to expose diagonal intersecting points. You may have to change the direction you pressed some prior seam allowances as you continue assembly.

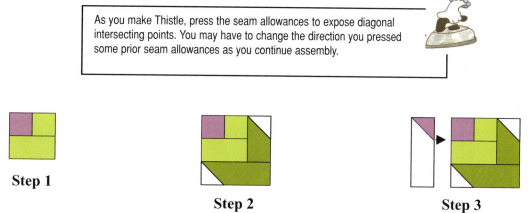

Step 1

Step 2

Step 3

Step 2: To make the rest of the flower, pin 2S patches right sides together at the correct ends of 2X4R and 2X6R, referring to your color diagram. **Be sure to draw the diagonal line in the proper direction.** Pin, sew, trim, and press. Then attach the 2X4R sub-unit to the right side of Unit 1. Press seam allowance toward Unit 1. Make and sew 2X6R sub-unit to the bottom of Unit 1 in the same way. Press the seam allowance also toward Unit 1.

Step 3: Make and add the 2X6R sub-unit that is part of the left edge of the block. When you are sewing this unit to Unit 1, you won't be able to see both diagonal and straight intersections. Use the hold pin technique. The hold pin insertion point denotes where the seam should be sewn.

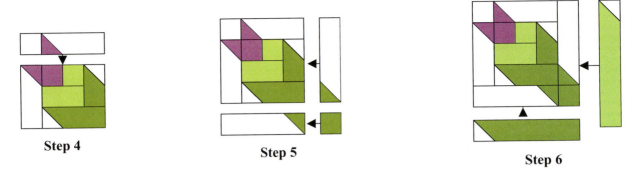

Step 4   **Step 5**   **Step 6**

Step 4: Make another 2X6R sub-unit, attach a 2S background patch and sew to the top edge of the block using the hold pin technique. You again have a square.

Step 5: Continue by making two 2X8R sub-units with 2S in the leaf color attached to the correct end of each rectangle. Attach 2S in the leaf color to the bottom sub-unit and sew to the block.

Step 6: Make the leaf sub-units which complete the block using 2X10R + 2S and 2X12R + 2S and attach.

Would you like to try another similar block all by yourself?

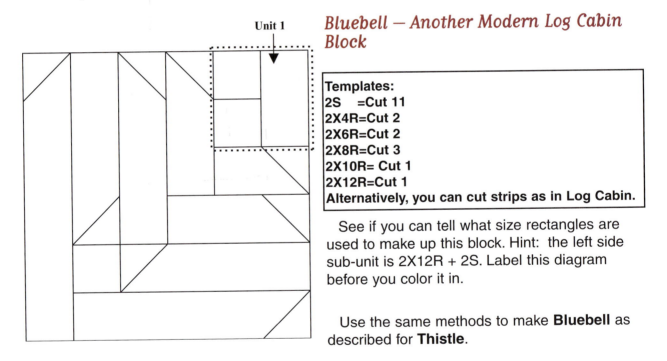

Unit 1

Bluebell — Another Modern Log Cabin Block

Templates:
2S   =Cut 11
2X4R=Cut 2
2X6R=Cut 2
2X8R=Cut 3
2X10R= Cut 1
2X12R=Cut 1
Alternatively, you can cut strips as in Log Cabin.

See if you can tell what size rectangles are used to make up this block. Hint: the left side sub-unit is 2X12R + 2S. Label this diagram before you color it in.

Use the same methods to make **Bluebell** as described for **Thistle**.

The "center" (Unit 1) for **Bluebell** is the three-patch unit in the upper right hand corner and consists of two 2S patches and one 2X4R rectangle. You use the half-square triangle technique to make each rectangle that you add alternately to the left and bottom sides of the block.

You're really making progress!

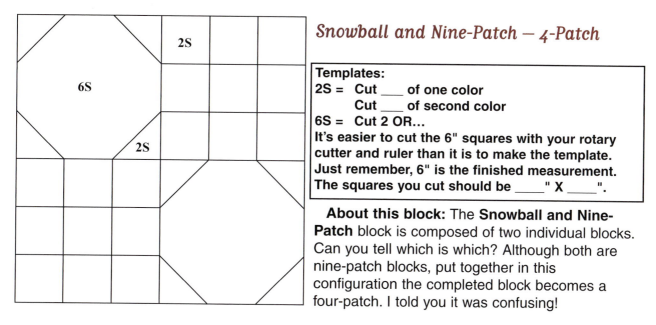

Snowball and Nine-Patch — 4-Patch

Templates:
2S = Cut ___ of one color
        Cut ___ of second color
6S = Cut 2 OR...
It's easier to cut the 6" squares with your rotary cutter and ruler than it is to make the template. Just remember, 6" is the finished measurement. The squares you cut should be ___" X ___".

About this block: The **Snowball and Nine-Patch** block is composed of two individual blocks. Can you tell which is which? Although both are nine-patch blocks, put together in this configuration the completed block becomes a four-patch. I told you it was confusing!

You already know the importance of coloring and referring to the diagram. You also have learned enough about what patches make up a block to be able to tell how many of each kind are in this block, including the extra eight 2S patches you will need to make the Snowballs.

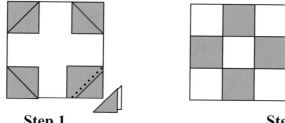

Step 1   **Steps 2 & 3**

Step 1: Let's make the Snowball Block first. You can see the corners of 6S are cut off diagonally in another application of the half-square triangle technique. Right sides together, squarely position a 2S patch at each corner of 6S. Make sure their two common edges are even. Pin within the half-square triangle you want to save. Draw the diagonal sewing line, sew, cut, and press. *Voila* – a snowball! Make two.

Step 2: The nine-patch is assembled in the same way as the **Four-Patch** block.

Step 3: Now for the difficult part. Using the holding pin technique, you have to match up diagonal seams with perpendicular seams as you join one nine-patch to a Snowball unit. Not only that, you have to join the resulting half blocks to each other and match even more diagonal to perpendicular seams. Using the holding pin technique should take most of the pain away ... and there's always the seam ripper to make corrections. Do the best you can, and don't forget "Creative Pressing."

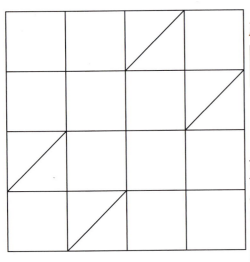

Road to Oklahoma

Template: 3S = Cut 20

All totaled, you will need twenty 3" squares.

Begin by making four half-square triangles.

Assemble the four, four-patch units. Two will be just like the **Four-Patch** block and two will contain half-square triangles. Always press for ease of construction, so you can see points and intersections when you are joining units.

Don't forget all the helpful techniques you've learned: pressing to nest, holding pin, creative pressing, imaginative seam allowances, etc.

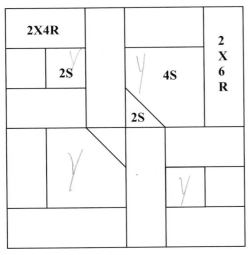

Loop the Loop

Templates:
2S = Cut 6
4S = Cut 2
2X4R = Cut 6   — 2" ✗ 4'
2X6R = Cut 4   2" ✗ 6 =

This block is a four-patch made up of two different units, as you can see in the line drawing. Magic happens when you make a whole quilt of this block, rotating one to another 1/4 turn as you sew the blocks together.

Assemble both like units then join together nesting seams and matching intersections.

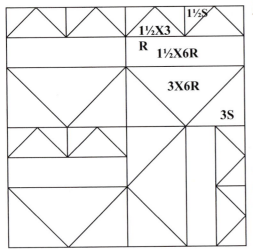

Four Hearts

Templates:
1-1/2S = Cut 162S = Cut 6
1-1/2X3R = Cut 8
1-1/2X6R = Cut 4
3X6R = Cut 4
3S = Cut 8

This is not an easy block —a cute block, yes, but not an easy one. You have the skills and the knowledge to make it. By the time you finish the fourth heart, you'll be an expert. Good luck!

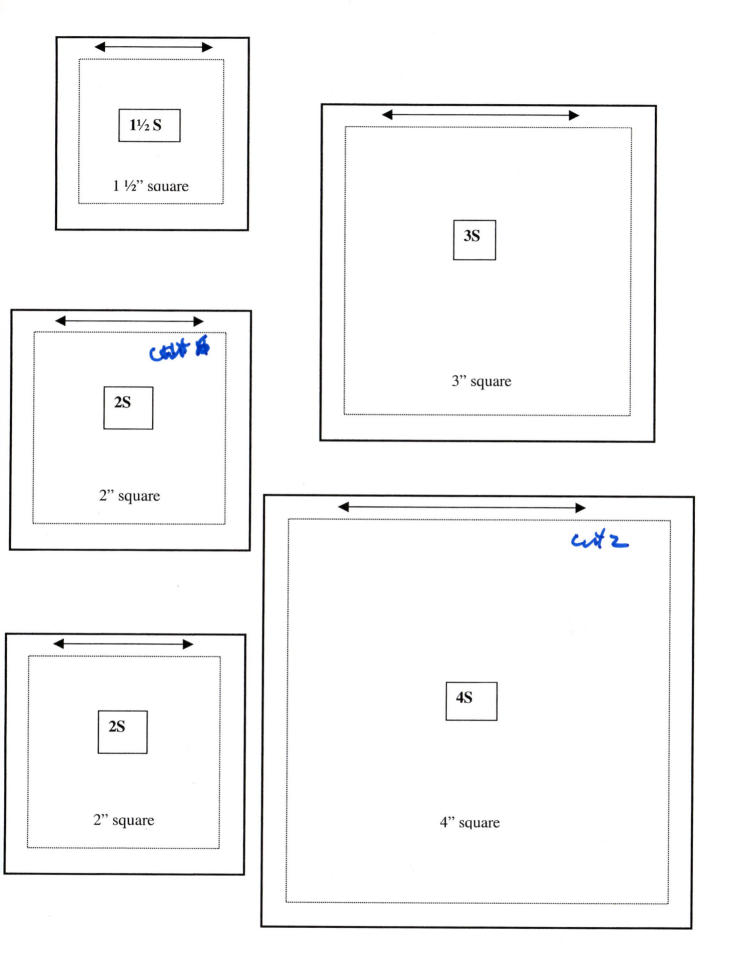

1½ S

1 ½" square

2S

cut 6

2" square

2S

2" square

3S

3" square

4S

cut 2

4" square

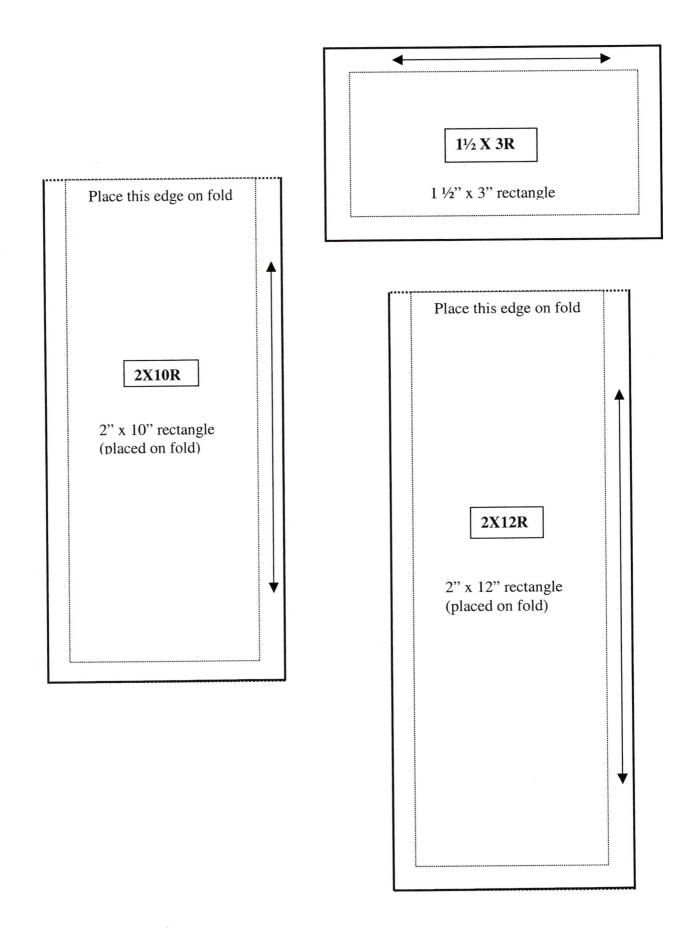

1½ X 3R

1 ½" x 3" rectangle

Place this edge on fold

2X10R

2" x 10" rectangle
(placed on fold)

Place this edge on fold

2X12R

2" x 12" rectangle
(placed on fold)

1½ X6R

1 ½" x 6" rectangle

2X6R

cut 4

2"X6" rectangle

4X6R

4" x 6" rectangle

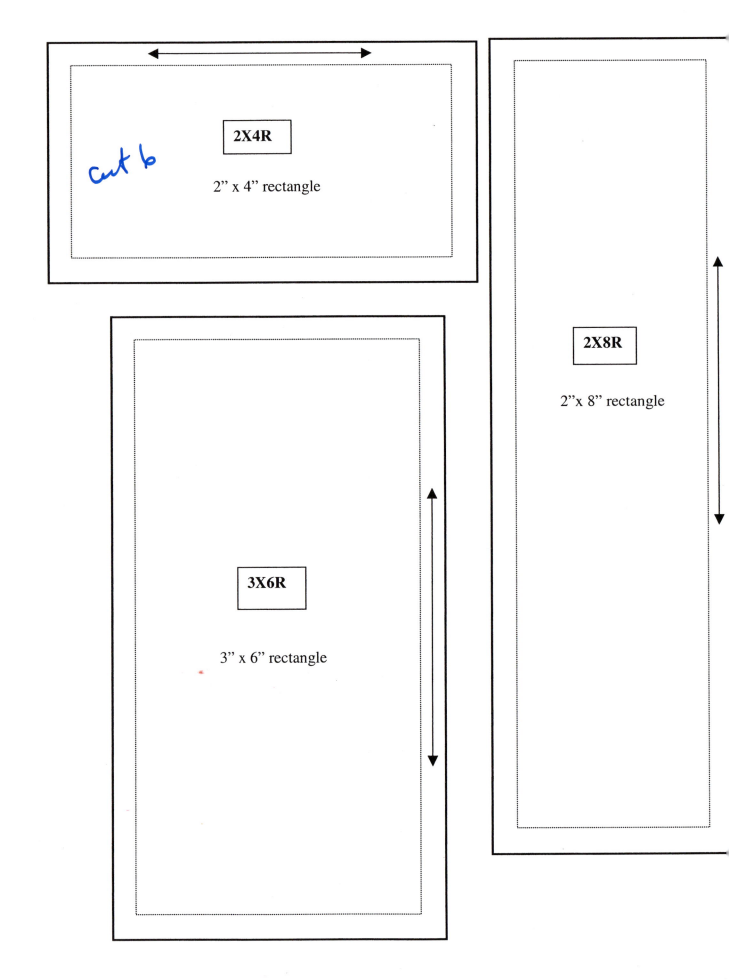

2X4R

2" x 4" rectangle

Cut 6

2X8R

2"x 8" rectangle

3X6R

3" x 6" rectangle

Remember, you don't have to make this large template if you don't want to.

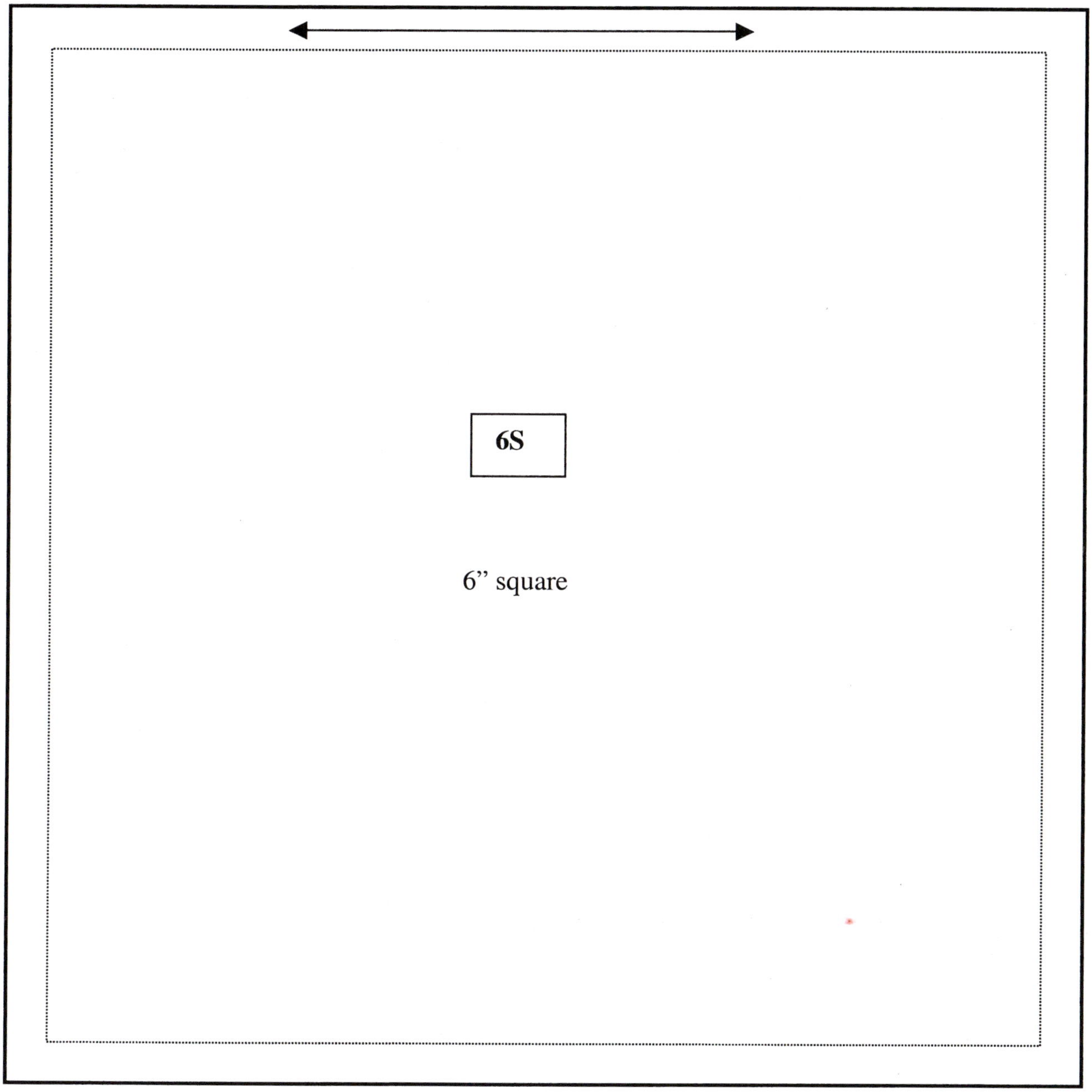

6S

6" square

Triangles
LESSON 4

Working with Triangles:
Try one of the blocks in this column first to practice working with bias.

These are all different arrangements of a basic block known as Variable Star.

Can you see that these three nine-patch blocks are very similar?

Here are the Challenge Triangle blocks:

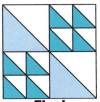

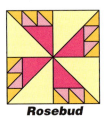

Flock

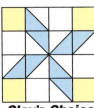

Clay's Choice

Ohio Star

54-50 or Fight

Rosebud

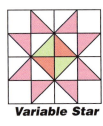

Variable Star

Sweet Gun Leaf

Tic-Tac-Toe

Dutchman's Puzzle

Broken Dishes

Card Trick

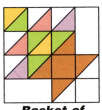

Basket of Triangles

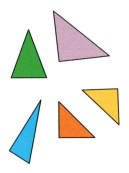

Pinwheel

The stem in Sweet Gum Leaf is made using freezer paper appliqué. You can learn how in this lesson.

Barbara Fritchie Star

Triangles

Triangle shapes used in patchwork are versatile. Blocks containing triangles can be used to show direction. They can be used together to create the illusion of curves. They come in so many happy three-sided shapes. They can be sturdy and solid, or they can be slender and graceful. You can see by the number of triangle blocks included in this lesson how much I enjoy working with them.

Sewing patchwork triangles can be a real challenge. In Lesson 3, you learned how to create triangle units using the half-square triangle method that eliminated the complications of working with patches that have side(s) cut on fabric bias. In this lesson you will learn how to deal with the idiosyncrasies of bias fabric. Don't be tempted to use the half-square triangle technique when constructing the blocks. It's important that you learn how to work with triangles' bias sides that, guaranteed, will easily stretch out of shape.

Do you remember where bias is in fabric? If not, go back to Lesson 3 to review. Although true bias runs at a 45 degree angle, any cut of fabric that is not on the lengthwise or crosswise grain should also be treated as bias because it, too, will stretch. I can't stress strongly enough that an understanding of the inherent characteristics of fabrics will help you use their idiosyncrasies to your advantage.

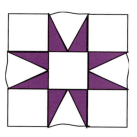

As mentioned before, whenever we cut fabric patches that will have bias side(s), we must think ahead to where the patch will appear in a sub-unit, unit, or even in a block. We do not want any bias on the outside edges of our blocks.

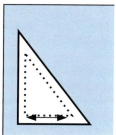

Our templates have arrows showing grainline to help you in orienting them on your fabric before cutting. By placing the templates on your fabric and aligning the arrows to either the crosswise or lengthwise grain, your patches will be cut correctly.

A Triangle is a Polygon with the Least Number of Sides

There are specific names for triangles of different shapes. They are classified by the angles they contain (see illustrations below).

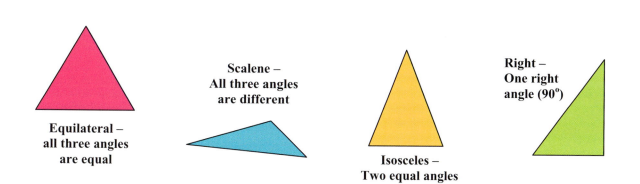

Equilateral –
all three angles
are equal

Scalene –
All three angles
are different

Isosceles –
Two equal angles

Right –
One right
angle (90⁰)

We will use the **Flock Block** as an example to demonstrate how to work with triangles. Three-inch and six-inch right triangles make up the block. Cut eight 3" triangles (3RT) from two fabrics. Cut four 6" triangles (6RT) from two fabrics.

Okay, let's go for those little 3" triangles. Overlay, right sides together, eight 2-color sets of 3RT. When joining these triangles, it is a simple matter to match all the angles. Pin your triangle patches together at the beginning and end of the seam line as shown. The pins act as "handles" for you to hold to keep the seam straight. This is especially important at the end of the seam where the patch will tend to move sideways as it exits the presser foot. Hold onto those handles removing them just before the needle reaches them.

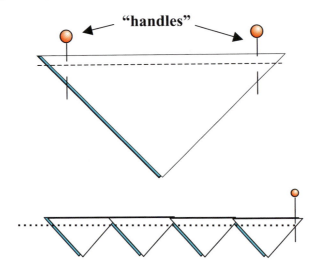

Now is a good time to use the chain piecing technique. As you guide the patches one after another between the presser foot and the feed dogs, slightly overlap the triangles (as shown). A continuous feed of fabric helps keep the patches from skewing sideways by giving the feed dogs something to "bite" onto. Enough thread is stitched between patches to make a secure seam. Don't forget to use your scrap "leaders" and "followers."

Use a stiletto, seam ripper, or sharpened wooden chopstick to help you hold those little patches as you sew.

After you have sewn all 3RT together, press seam allowances of six sub-units in one direction and the seam allowance of the other two sub-units in the other direction. This will allow you to see intersections when you join them together later.

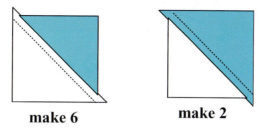

make 6   make 2

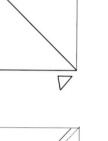

After pressing, you will see that you have little triangles overhanging at the seam. I call these "bunny ears" (what else?). Trim off the overhanging "ears" to make a square. (Some quilters prefer to cut off the bunny ears prior to assembly. I don't; I use those little triangular tips to help me correctly align patches.)

Next, sew the 3RT sub-units together as you did when you made the **Four-Patch** block. Be sure to employ the "hold" pin technique you learned in the last lesson. You'll notice this unit is quite similar to one in **Road to Oklahoma**, but you have twice the number of diagonal-to-straight seam intersections to match. Make two four-patch units.

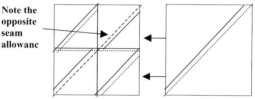

Note the opposite seam allowanc

Reverse sides

Make two 6RT triangle squares. Press the diagonal seams opposite each other and attach to the correct side of each four-patch unit.

Sew the two block halves together, nesting and matching seams. Use your "imaginative seam allowance" trick, if necessary. "Creative press" the final seam join to get the best look on the right side. You're done!

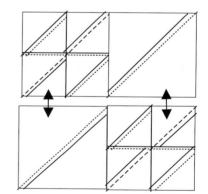

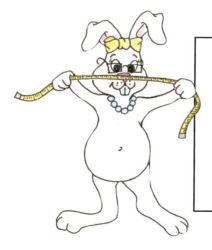

As you continue piecing each block, always check the dimensions of your assembled units to see if they "measure up" to the pattern.

When joining triangles to assembled units that take on a new shape, as in the **Rosebud Block,** you will have to *offset* your patches by the 1/4" seam allowance. This exemplifies why I don't like to trim the bunny ears off my triangles before sewing; those little corners help you judge where to set your patches and place your seam.

Rosebud is made from 2", 4", and 6" right triangles. To begin, sew two sets of 2RT together on the long side as shown for **Flock** making two squares. Orient the colors correctly, and join the two squares to make a rectangle. Don't forget to use your "handles."

As you look at your rectangle sub-unit, check your colored-in pattern to determine which side to attach 4RT. Overlay the 4RT patch matching right angles and offsetting the overhanging corner by *approximately* 1/4". Pin, and sew beginning at the offset. Trim the bunny ear as shown, and press the seam allowance to the darker color (or the direction that makes your piecing look the best).

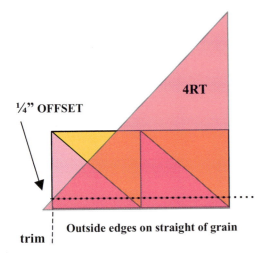

¼" OFFSET

4RT

trim

Outside edges on straight of grain

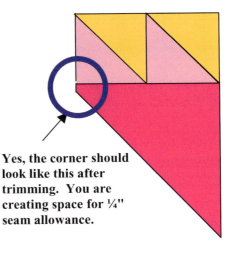

Yes, the corner should look like this after trimming. You are creating space for ¼" seam allowance.

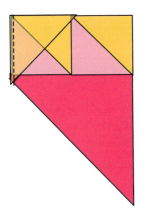

In the same way you attached 4RT, attach another 2RT to the left edge of the rectangle sub-unit matching right angles and offsetting the overhanging corner by approximately 1/4". You can trim the offset angle, but it's not necessary if you press the seam allowance toward the pieced rectangle. It should fall in line with the long side of 4RT.

This is how your pieced triangle should look when completed. Notice there appears to be an extension on the long side of the assembled unit that allows for the ¼" seam.

Making one-fourth of the **Rosebud** block is a simple matter of sewing two 6RT together, one pieced by **you**. Make three more and sew them together matching and nesting seams as shown for **Flock**, and your block will be done. You'll be getting lots of experience using imaginative seam allowances and creative pressing for practically perfect patchwork.

There are two more types of seams encountered when piecing triangle blocks in this lesson.

The diagram below shows bias sides of two differently shaped triangles being sewn together. You will encounter this configuration in **Dutchman's Puzzle**, and **54-40 or Fight**. When sewing

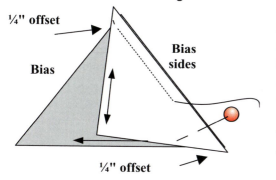

these types of patches together, offset and pin the two end points, then stitch while holding the seam taut. (I won't use the word "pulling." What you want to do is keep the raw edges even and patches aligned as you sew.) This type of unit is an example of the "no outside bias edges" rule. Remember, if one of the patches is extra stretchy; sew with it on the bottom against the feed dogs. Let the feed dogs do the easing in.

Tic-Tac-Toe brings you another type of triangle seam to conquer. Compared to sewing two bias triangle sides together, this seam is a cinch! For clarity, the diagram shows the triangle being sewn on top, but give the feed dogs on your machine something to do by placing the triangle under the square for stitching.

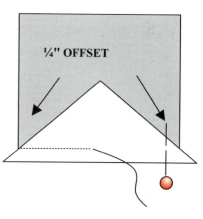

Again, at times you might have to alter the direction you pressed a seam when you sew your completed units into blocks. You'll be creating "floating" seam allowances within some of the blocks in this lesson.

Homework

The patterns and instructions for Lesson 4 – Triangles, follow. Your assignment in developing triangle block-making skills is:

- Complete your choice of **Flock**, **Rosebud**, or **Dutchman's Puzzle**.
- Choose and make a variable star block from those shown on page 50. All the variable star adaptations are more intricate versions of the **Four-Patch** block we learned in Lesson 3.
- Make one of the Nine-patch blocks: **Ohio Star**, **Card Trick**, or **Sweet Gum Leaf**.
- *Optional*: Choose, and make, one of the Challenge Blocks: **Tic-Tac-Toe** (not such a challenge), **54-40 or Fight,** or **Basket of Triangles**.
- Make templates for Lesson 5, Polygons.

> Refer back to your chosen quilt diagram to see if you're on track in the number of quilt blocks you will need to finish your quilt. I've found that you will want to make more blocks than required because some just won't look that good with the rest. You can make pillows out of the orphans.

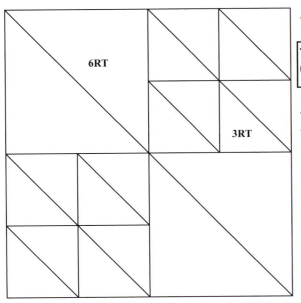

Flock

> **Templates: 3RT = Cut 8 of two colors**
> **6RT = Cut 2 of two colors**

About this block: The quilter who made up this four-patch block must have loved watching the birds flock up to fly South for the winter. She reduced her piecing work by substituting one large 6" triangle for four smaller 3" triangles. (There were many chores early quiltmakers had to do besides making all their family bedcovers.)

Using the color example, choose your fabrics to contrast well so you can see the "flying birds" design.

Arrange and assemble as you learned in this lesson.

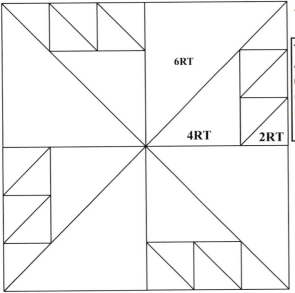

Rosebud

> **Templates: 2RT = Cut 20 of two colors**
> **4RT = Cut 4**
> **6RT = Cut 4**
> **Okay, you can use 2S for the half-square triangles, I'll never know. But don't cheat yourself in learning how to piece the smaller triangles.**

About this block: This large pinwheel-type block is another four-patch variation.

Using the instructions in this lesson, assemble the four units positioning each unit a quarter turn from the one next to it.

POWER CHECKLIST

√ *Chain piecing*
√ *Press to nest*
√ *Match points with imaginative seam allowances*
√ *Creative press for the best look*

√ *Measure completed units for accuracy*
√ *Use "hold" pin*
√ *Trim bunny ears*

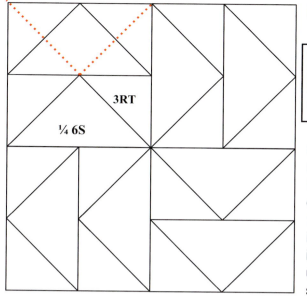

Dutchman's Puzzle

Templates: 1/4 6S = Cut 8
3RT = Cut 16
Experiment with your color choices to create a secondary pinwheel pattern.

About this block: Even though template 1/4 6S is a right triangle, what it is **not,** as you can see, is half a square as used in this block. 1/4 6S is a triangle you get when you divide a square diagonally with an "X". It's **a fourth** of a square. 1/4 6S is smaller than 6RT. The patches aren't interchangeable. This example shows the importance of knowing whether a triangle is used as half of a square or a quarter of a square.

Step 1: Cut eight 1/4 6S with the longest side on the straight of grain. Cut 16 of 3RT with right angle sides on straight of grain.

Step 2: To make the rectangular sub-unit, stitch 3RT to both short sides of 1/4 6S using the handle and offset techniques shown in the lesson. This is another good time to do your chain piecing. Make eight pieced rectangles. Press seams to 3RT.

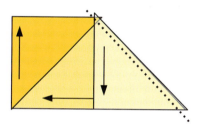

Step 3: Stitch two rectangle sub-units together using the imaginative seam technique, if necessary. As you join the sub-units, you want to have your seam line cross just above the apex of 1/4 6S (see circle in diagram below) to make a perfect intersection. Use creative pressing to get the best look. You can readjust the seam allowance to expose the outside angle when sewing the units together. Remember, always sew with the points you are trying to match visible on top. In this way, make four units.

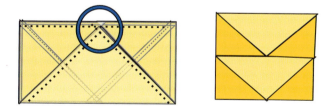

You won't see this target point

But you will see these two

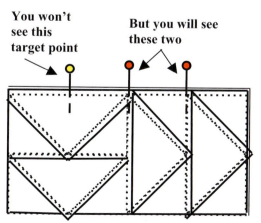

Step 4: Adjust and create floating seam allowances as you pin and get ready to sew the two halves. You will only be able to see two target intersections on the top unit. Nest and use a hold pin for the exact middle intersection and the visible target point. Place another pin to indicate the hidden target point and stitch the seam.

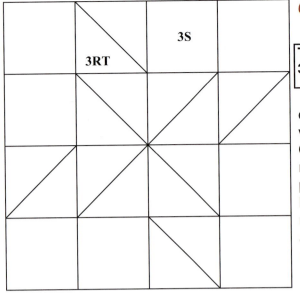

Clay's Choice

Templates: 3RT = Cut 16
3S = Cut 8

About these blocks: The five four-patch blocks on this page and the next are classified as variations of the **Variable Star** block. **Clay's Choice** and **Variable Star** have triangle shapes replaced by squares, thus reducing the number of patches. **Barbara Fritchie Star, Pinwheel,** and **Broken Dishes** are only three examples of the many patterns you can make by altering the arrangement and coloration of the triangle patches.

You have the skills to make any of these five blocks. They are shown in order of difficulty. Just remember your helpers: chain piecing, trimming bunny ears, "hold pin," matching points with imaginative seam allowances, floating seams, pressing to nest, and creative pressing for the best look.

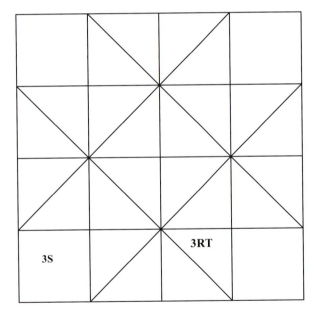

Variable Star

Templates: 3S = Cut 4
3RT = Cut 24

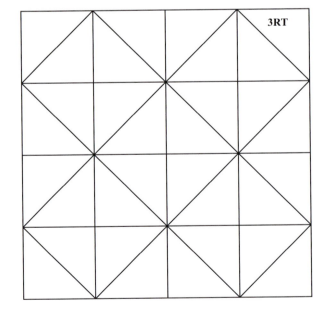

Broken Dishes

Template: 3RT = Cut 32

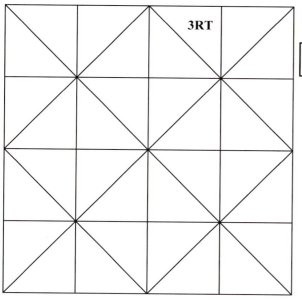

3RT

Pinwheel

Template: 3RT = Cut 32

Aren't you glad we have rotary cutters?

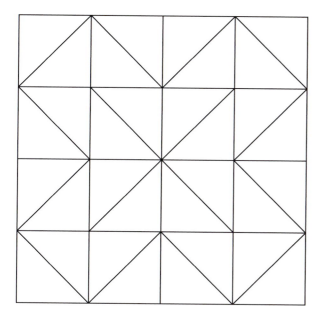

Barbara Fritchie Star

Templates: 3RT = Cut 32

You're a Star!

Templates: Make up your own block.

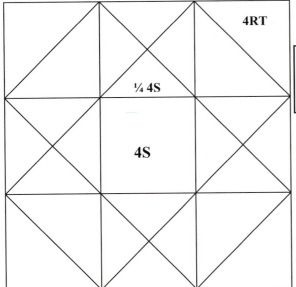

Ohio Star

Templates:
1/4 4S = Cut 16
4RT = Cut 4
4S = Cut 1

About this block: Although similar, this star differs from the **Variable Star** in that it's a nine-patch instead of a four-patch block. After piecing 16 sub-units, you'll appreciate making only nine for this block – and the center square is **not** pieced!

Remember correct cutting placement of the long side of 1/4 4S to keep outside edges on the straight of grain.

Card Trick

Templates:
4RT = Cut 12
1/4 4S = Cut 12

About this block: Yet another block that uses 1/4 square triangles. Note the placement of the long side of 1/4 4S. It always appears as the outside edge of the unit/block, so you know you'll have to cut those triangles with the long side on the straight of grain. **Card Trick** is a variation of **Ohio Star**. Broken down into its component parts, you can see how easy it is to construct. Use of color here is very important to achieve the illusion of interlocking "cards."

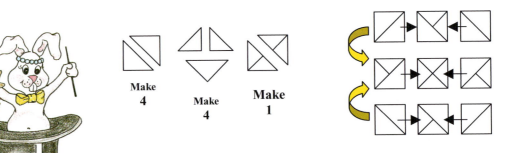

Make 4   Make 4   Make 1

Refer to diagrams as you assemble sub-units.

Sweet Gum Leaf

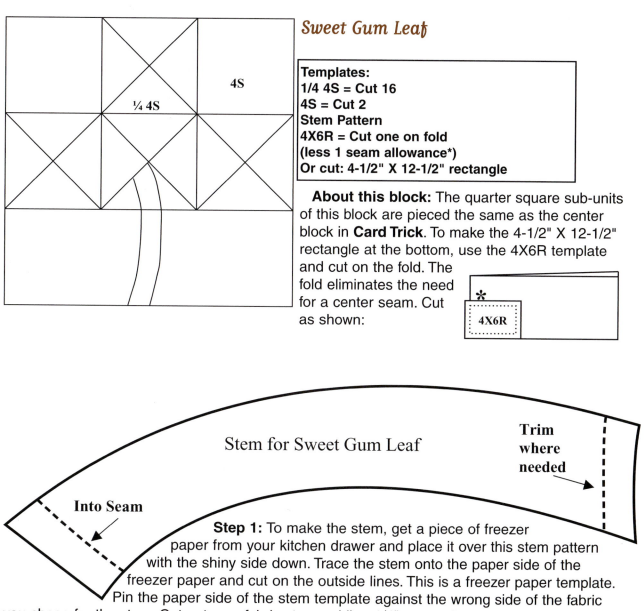

Templates:
1/4 4S = Cut 16
4S = Cut 2
Stem Pattern
4X6R = Cut one on fold
(less 1 seam allowance*)
Or cut: 4-1/2" X 12-1/2" rectangle

About this block: The quarter square sub-units of this block are pieced the same as the center block in **Card Trick**. To make the 4-1/2" X 12-1/2" rectangle at the bottom, use the 4X6R template and cut on the fold. The fold eliminates the need for a center seam. Cut as shown:

*

4X6R

Stem for Sweet Gum Leaf

Trim where needed

Into Seam

Step 1: To make the stem, get a piece of freezer paper from your kitchen drawer and place it over this stem pattern with the shiny side down. Trace the stem onto the paper side of the freezer paper and cut on the outside lines. This is a freezer paper template. Pin the paper side of the stem template against the wrong side of the fabric you chose for the stem. Cut out your fabric stem, adding 1/4" seam allowances to the two long sides.

Step 2: With your iron on the "dry" setting, press the fabric seam allowances over onto the shiny side of the freezer paper. It will stick, yet won't leave any residue on the patch: you have just made freezer paper applique.

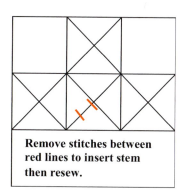

Remove stitches between red lines to insert stem then resew.

Step 3: To sew the stem in place, remove stitching between the red lines shown in the diagram. Insert the raw edge of one stem end, position it, and pin the stem in place.

Step 4: Replace the top thread in your machine with a color that matches the stem. Sew the stem to the block on both long sides as close as you can to the outside edges. Pull out the freezer paper template.

Step 5: Sew the insertion point closed through the stem end; how about that?

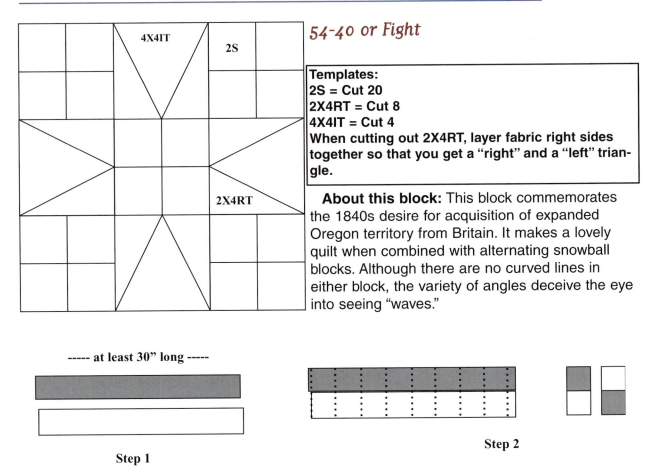

54-40 or Fight

Templates:
2S = Cut 20
2X4RT = Cut 8
4X4IT = Cut 4
When cutting out 2X4RT, layer fabric right sides together so that you get a "right" and a "left" triangle.

About this block: This block commemorates the 1840s desire for acquisition of expanded Oregon territory from Britain. It makes a lovely quilt when combined with alternating snowball blocks. Although there are no curved lines in either block, the variety of angles deceive the eye into seeing "waves."

----- at least 30" long -----

Step 1

Step 2

Step 1: For an easy way to get the four-patch blocks, use the strip piecing technique. This time you will cut two strips about 30" long by 2-1/2" wide.

Step 2: After you've sewn two strips together on the long side, slice off already-assembled rectangle units that measure 2-1/2" X 4-1/2". Reverse one, and place two pieced rectangles right sides together, nest seams, and sew to make the four-patch sub-unit.

Step 3: To make the triangle subunits, offset the small angle on 2X4RT by 1/4" (approximately – it's bias; it stretches). The angle of 2X4RT will match the angle of 4X4IT at the apex for 1/4".

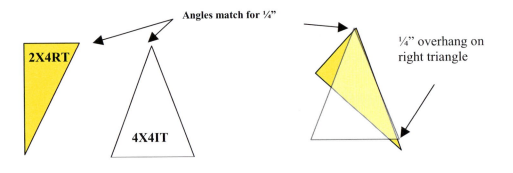

Angles match for ¼"

2X4RT

4X4IT

¼" overhang on right triangle

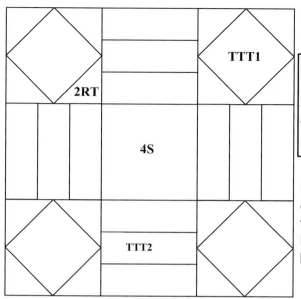

Tic-Tac-Toe

Templates:		
4S = Cut 1		
2RT = Cut 16		
Tic-Tac-Toe1 = Cut 4		
Tic-Tac-Toe 2 = Cut 12		
Or: make strips, sew, and cut		

About this block: Tic-Tac-Toe is a fun block to make and is graphically interesting. It reminds me of a game board. You can use the same shortcut to make the "bar" units as you did for **Hole in the Barn Door.** Cut the unfinished strips 1-7/8" wide by approximately 20" long.

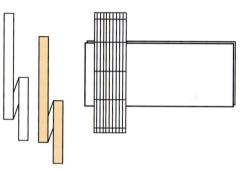

Basket of Triangles

Templates:		
3RT = Cut 16		
6RT = Cut 2		
3X6R = Cut 2		

About this block: The challenge of **Basket of Triangles** is in matching seam intersections. Join the basket to the triangle "flowers" to make a square. Then attach the background with basket base ends. Finally, add the 6RT corner background.

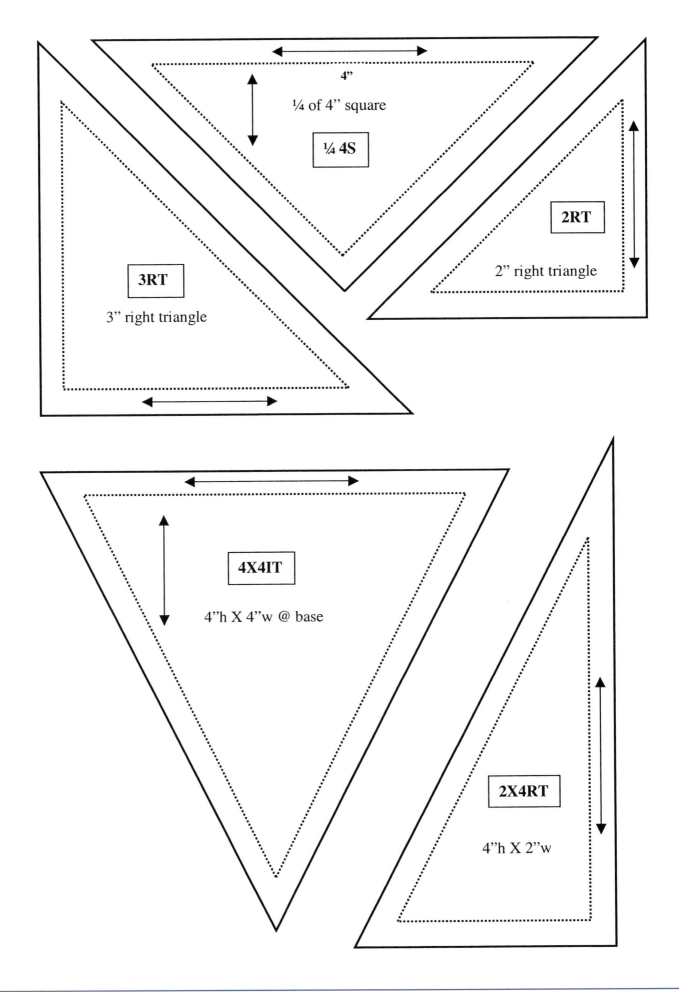

¼ of 4" square

¼ 4S

2RT

2" right triangle

3RT

3" right triangle

4X4IT

4"h X 4"w @ base

2X4RT

4"h X 2"w

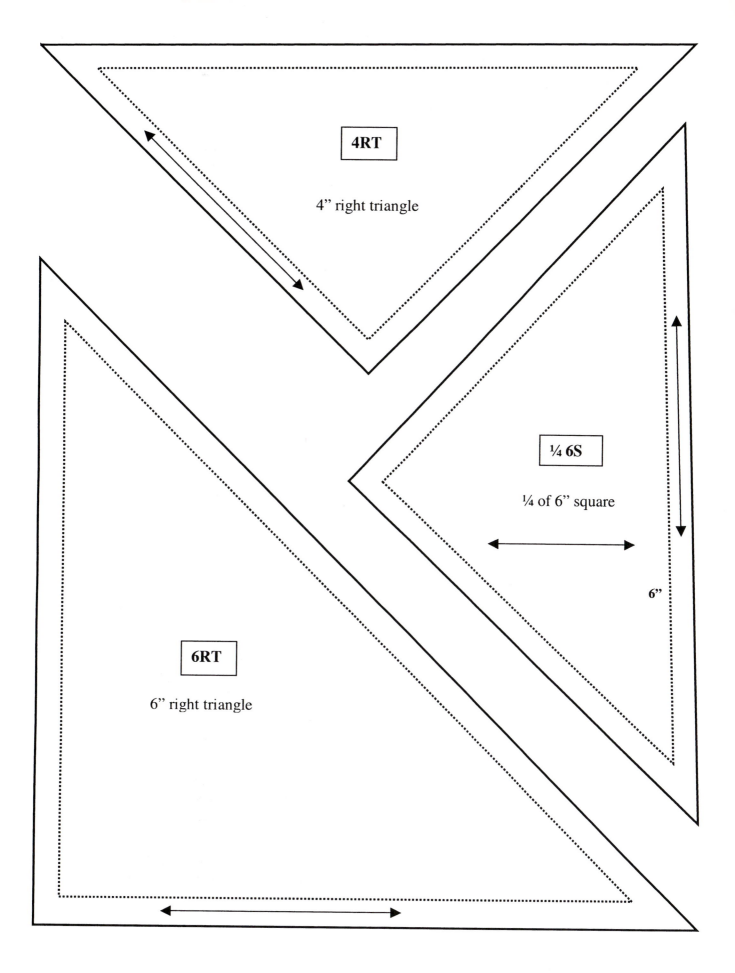

4RT

4" right triangle

¼ 6S

¼ of 6" square

6"

6RT

6" right triangle

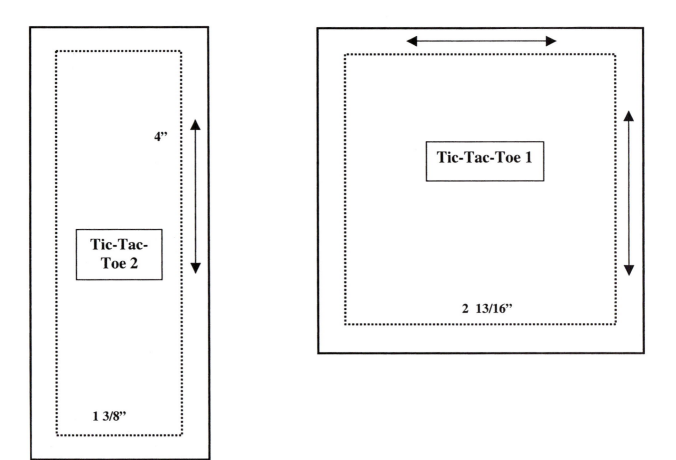

Tic-Tac-Toe 2

4"

1 3/8"

Tic-Tac-Toe 1

2 13/16"

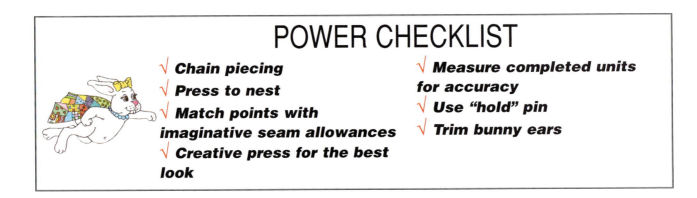

POWER CHECKLIST

√ **Chain piecing**
√ **Press to nest**
√ **Match points with imaginative seam allowances**
√ **Creative press for the best look**

√ **Measure completed units for accuracy**
√ **Use "hold" pin**
√ **Trim bunny ears**

LESSON 5

Parallelograms resemble two joined right triangles. They reduce the number of patches and seams. But _watch out_: there are left ones and right ones!

Trapezoids join squares or rectangles with triangles and also can be directional

Challenges

Joined Variable Star

Bouquet of Flowers

Spools

Bow Tie

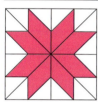

Windblown Square

Flower Pot

Next-Door Neighbor

House on the Hill

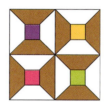

Shooting Star

8-Pointed Star

Light and Shadow

Diamonds are like two joined isosceles triangles If you can successfully sew blocks containing diamonds, there isn't any patchwork block you won't be able to conquer!

Alsace Lorraine

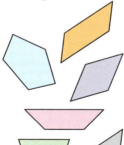

What's a Polygon

Webster's definition of a polygon is "a closed plane figure bound by straight lines." We have specific names for the most common polygons.

Square

Rectangle

Triangle

Diamond

Parallelogram

Trapezoid

Pentagon

Hexagon

Octagon

Many of these shapes appear as templates in this guide. You have already conquered squares and triangles, so let's move on to the specific polygon shapes of diamond, parallelogram, trapezoid, and pentagon introduced in this lesson.

I view all polygons as timesavers in cutting and sewing patchwork by reducing the number of patches needed to construct a block. They are combinations of the simpler shapes we have already mastered. Their larger area allows for more opportunities to create design interest. You can use larger prints for these patches, and they can provide a canvas for your quilting motifs. In this lesson you will even learn how to manipulate a diamond template to create a type of kaleidoscope block.

As you grow in your understanding of patchwork design, you'll want to create your own blocks. Being able to break shapes down into easy-to-draw figures will help you transfer your ideas into patterns. All you'll need is graph paper, a pencil, and a ruler.

Generally, the more complicated the shape, the more skill required to assemble it into blocks. We'll discover new techniques and tricks as we build upon construction methods you have already learned. *You can do it!*

Parallelograms

Looking at the blocks for this lesson on page 67, you can see they are grouped in rows according to the skill to be learned, with three additional blocks offered as challenges. The blocks in the first row contain parallelograms, which are the easiest of these new shapes to sew. Be careful, though: Parallelograms are devious. There are right- and left-facing varieties.

Look at the four parallelograms in **Windblown Square**. They are all the same shape facing in the same direction. That means you have to cut your patches with the right side of your fabric facing up.

The parallelogram patches on **Shooting Star** likewise are the same shape facing in the same direction, but not the same direction as Windblown Square. These patches are "reverse," and must be cut with the right side of your fabric facing down.

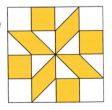

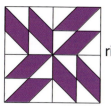

How would you cut the eight parallelograms for **Alsace Lorraine?** That's right; they would all be cut on the right side of the fabric.

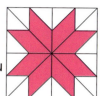

How would you cut the parallelograms for **Joined Variable Star**? Here you're safe, because there are an equal number of right and left parallelograms, so you cut these patches as you normally would, with wrong sides of your fabric facing each other.

You probably noticed as you made the templates for Lesson 5 that some were labeled "# & #R." Adding an "R" designation to a template means it is also used in "reverse" for left- and right-facing patches. When cutting, you reverse the fabric not the template.

Making Parallelogram Units

Joined Variable Star is a good block to begin working with parallelograms because you can cut eight PAL1 & 1R from your fabric in the usual way (with wrong sides together). Remember, this gives you right and left facing patches. You will also cut sixteen 3RT patches.

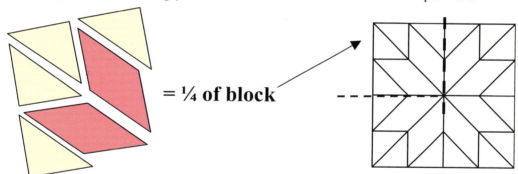

= ¼ of block

To this day, I find working with right/left parallelograms to be confusing, so I always lay out my patches as they should be assembled, using the line drawing in the pattern section as a guide.

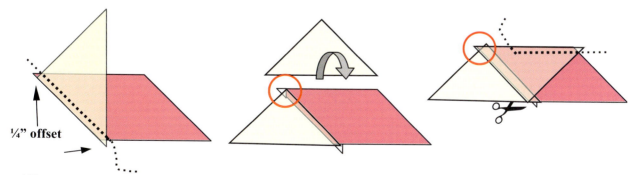

¼" offset

We will apply the offset technique we learned in Lesson 4, and treat the diagonally-cut ends of parallelograms as triangles to be offset when attached to another patch. Join 3RT to PAL 1&1R, right sides together, offsetting the two angles as shown. Press the seam allowances away from PAL 1 to expose point intersections for later matching. *Don't* clip bunny ears yet.

Use the offset bunny ear shown in the red circle to help you place the next 3RT onto the sub-unit. Just match the angles with right sides together, offset the opposite angle, and sew the seam. If easing is necessary, sew with the difficult patch against the feed dogs. Again you can see why I don't like templates that already have their bunny ears cropped. Now you can trim bunny ears and press the seam allowance toward the triangle.

Are we having fun yet? We've learned to make a larger pieced triangle out of two smaller triangles and a parallelogram. Sew one more as a mirror image of the unit you just made.

By pressing seam allowances away from the parallelogram, the seam crossing point at the edge of the block is exposed and the block will lie flat when finished—but we have created a problem for ourselves: how are we going to join these two units since there are no cross seams to reference or opposing seam allowances to nest? You could readjust your seam allowances into floating seams so they do nest (and risk the block not lying flat), or we can use our helpful holding pin technique.

Invisible Matching Points

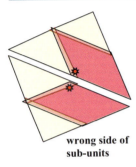

wrong side of sub-units

I'll bet you didn't know you had the skill to sew a perfect intersection without nesting seam allowances. The trick is in finding where the stitching *should* cross a seam. On the wrong side of both patches, use your rotary ruler (it's nice to have a small 6" one by the same manufacturer for things like this) to measure 1/4" in from the outside edge. Mark those points on the **seam** with a pencil or disappearing fabric marker.

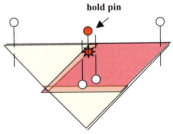

hold pin

Next, line up your patches, right sides together. Take a pin and insert it through the first mark then through to the mark on the second patch. Keep this hold pin perpendicular, and pin on either side, as usual.

Attach your handles to the ends of the triangle and sew the seam crossing over the invisible matching point. Don't remove the hold pin until your machine needle is almost on top of it. Press this seam to the left. You've successfully made one quarter of the **Joined Variable Star** block! Repeat these steps three more times to get four units.

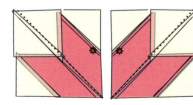

To join two of the four units together, again find the invisible matching points, mark, pin, and stitch the perpendicular seam. Press this seam to one side. Sew the other two blocks together, but press the perpendicular seam in the opposite direction for nesting.

Because you pressed the diagonal seams all in one direction and made opposing perpendicular seams, the two block halves will nest.

Use the hold pin technique at all matching points, including the center, to finish your block.

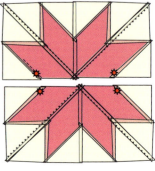

Since you can make the **Joined Variable Star** block, you'll also be able to make **Windblown Square, Shooting Star,** and **Alsace Lorraine.** The patterns for these, and all the other polygon blocks begin on page 76.

Diamonds are a Quilter's Best Friend

Diamonds are especially *my* best friend. When our youngest child was about 12, I went back to work (like taking care of a family and a home isn't work!). While this job was an opportunity to help my kids through college, it represented a loss of quilting time. I did get to make a few quick projects, most of which were baby quilts that were given away. Fifteen years later, my husband and I were involved in a car accident that aggravated an old neck injury I'd nursed for 20 years, and I eventually had to quit working.

Coincidentally, the same year I "retired," Viking Sewing Machines and JoAnn Fabric Stores co-sponsored a quilt contest entitled, "Diamonds are Forever." Entries had to relate to diamonds, and I entered the contest as a personal challenge to see if I could even complete a quilt that would qualify for the first prize—a Lily Viking sewing machine, which I certainly needed because my old machine was wearing out.

With my family's encouragement I persevered, making my entry for the contest. It was the first time in my life I gave myself permission to try to achieve a goal of my own. Well, long story short, my "Quilt Queen of Diamonds" won the grand prize … the beautiful Lily sewing machine. My family and I were thrilled.

While I waited for delivery from the manufacturer, one day I decided to visit my local sewing shop to see what the Lily looked like. The store had been notified that someone in its sales area had won the contest. When I went in, of course they first tried to sell me a new machine, but I told them I had won one. They asked if I was the winner of the "Diamonds are Forever" contest, then they asked me if I'd ever thought about teaching quilting. They offered me an opportunity to teach classes in their shop!

And that's how this book was born—because I wanted to teach quilting the way I wish I had learned. I sent my students home with handouts to help refresh their memories of class content; at the end of the 8-week session, I had a lot of handouts! One of my students said, "You ought to write a book." So I did. And that was the beginning of my wonderful new life.

Here is "Quilt Queen" to which I owe so much.

Okay, enough sidebar … let's get back to work!

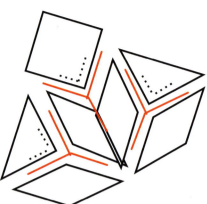

Blocks containing diamonds are among the more difficult to sew. Stitching diamond shapes to each other is tricky, and attaching the background patches presents an entirely different challenge. Each background square and triangle must be "set in." What is set in? If you sew clothing, you know that sleeves can be set in. Gussets can be set in. So can bound buttonholes and pockets. In patchwork, setting in means that two patches are sewn together, leaving space (seam allowance partly sewn) for insertion of a third patch so that no seams cross. All patches fit together and the block lies flat. This is accomplished by what is known as a "Y" seam.

Looking at the "Y" diagram here, wouldn't it be easier to assemble these patches by using right triangles? Then you'd just sew triangles to the sides of the diamonds and assemble the block like **Joined Variable Star.** You can do that, but if you follow a few simple rules, "Y" seams aren't that difficult, and having this skill in your repertoire will open a world of design possibilities. Besides, fewer seams make for better-looking blocks and save piecing, and that's what we're learning in this lesson of combined shapes.

Let's use **Bouquet of Flowers** to illustrate the construction of a diamond block with "Y" seams. Bouquet is a variation of the traditional **Eight-Pointed Star** block. It combines two of the diamonds into a polygon handle, and it offers the opportunity to work with three different set-in shapes.

As always, it is a good plan to color the line drawing on the pattern on page 77 with your fabric colors. This helps you organize the block patches. Begin by cutting six 12D diamonds from different fabrics. You can stack pieces of your fabrics and cut once. Also cut three 3-1/2 S, two 1/4 5S and two BF2 from the chosen background fabric. Cut one BF1 for the handle.

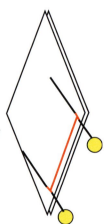

There is a trick to be learned about sewing diamond patches together. You just can't sew a 1/4" seam when joining two diamonds. I think it has something to do with all that bias. If you make perfect 1/4" seams, when you sew the last diamond to the first, you'll get a bump in the middle. So you have to "adjust" the seam allowance, *and* you also have to prepare those diamonds to set in the background patches.

Here we go! On the wrong side of three diamond patches, use your grid ruler and pencil or fabric marker to draw the seam allowance line (shown in red on the diagram). Draw only the seam line and indicate where it should start and stop 1/4" in from the outside edges. Since two patches are layered and sewn together, you only need to mark half the diamonds. Employ the "handle" trick by pinning patches together at the ends of the drawn seam line to help you see where these points are when you sew.

Starting at the widest part of the diamond, sew three sets of diamonds together, backstitching at the beginning and end of each drawn seam line. Begin with the machine needle touching the right side of the drawn line. As you sew, guide the patches so that the machine needle crosses over the drawn line halfway point and finishes touching the **left** side of the line. **The dotted line in the diagram is an exaggeration to show you seam placement.**

The object is to make a slightly wider seam at the block center where the diamond points join. This minor manipulation will ensure no bump in the middle of your joined diamonds. After you've made three of these two-diamond sets, press the seams open. **This is one of the few instances in which you will press the seams open to reduce bulk at the center of the block.**

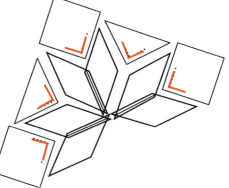

Now for the "Y" seam. In the same way you drew the seam line on the diamonds, draw the **corner** seam lines on the wrong sides of the squares and triangles. You don't need to draw the whole line because here you can stitch to the outside edge.

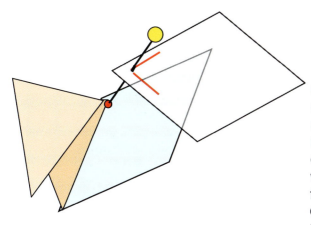

Last stitch hole is represented by red dot.

To set in the corner squares, adjust the left diamond out of the way, and overlay the square on the right diamond with right sides together as shown. Insert a pin where the drawn seam lines meet in the corner of the square. Since the diamonds are free from each other for 1/4", you will be able to continue inserting that pin into the first stitch hole you made on the right diamond. Offset the narrow end point of the diamond with the square and pin.

Starting at the center of the "Y", drop the machine needle into the last stitch hole as you pull out the pin, make a few forward stitches, backstitch, and sew the square to the right diamond, sewing off the raw edge.

Flip the square around and match raw edges to the second diamond. Adjust the first diamond patch out of the way and insert the pin into the first stitch hole in the corner of the square then into the stitch hole on the second diamond. You will sew this seam with the wrong side of the diamond facing up. Again, drop the machine needle into the first stitch hole, stitch, backstitch, and sew from the center out. Press seams toward the square so that you can see the point intersections when you assemble the block into your quilt.

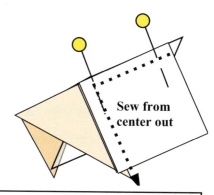

Sew from center out

The reason we have to backstitch set-in seams is that they really get a workout during assembly. If we don't secure the beginning and ending stitching, the little patches would pull apart and our blocks could be ruined.

After you have inset all the squares, sew the three diamond units together as before—only on the seam lines, backstitch at the beginning and ending of the seam. Press the seam allowances open.

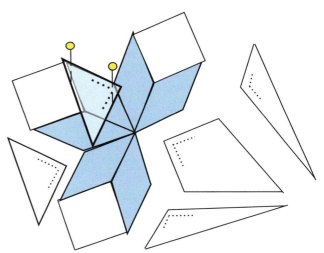

The triangle background patches and the handle are set in exactly as you did the squares. After you've set them in, attach the long background triangles to finish the block also using the set-in method.

Press all set-in seam allowances away from the diamonds. The diamond points on the wrong side of the very center of the block will open and twirl in a kind of pinwheel shape. Just touch the center with the tip of your iron to flatten.

Trapezoids

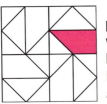

There are two types of trapezoids to learn in this lesson. One looks like a parallelogram missing one triangle end, and appears in **Next-Door Neighbor** where it is joined to a triangle. You don't know it, but you're already the expert here. All you have to do is match the long triangle side to the trapezoid angle. Do you recognize the combination? Yes, it is exactly the same way the triangle and parallelogram are sewn together in **Joined Variable Star**. The resulting sub-unit can then be treated as what it has become—a rectangle.

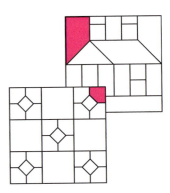

The trapezoids appearing in **House on the Hill** are also shaped like parallelograms missing one triangle end, but are set in as you have learned working with diamonds. See the specific pattern instructions at the end of this lesson to make both of these blocks.

The trapezoids in **Spools** and the pentagon "bow" in **Bow tie** are not the same shape, yet the same setting-in technique is used to make their blocks. Because the patches are larger, we will use **Spools** to learn how to set in trapezoids.

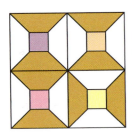

For this block you will need to cut four 2S and sixteen TRAP2. Color in the pattern at the back of this lesson with your fabric colors and keep it in front of you to help with patch placement.

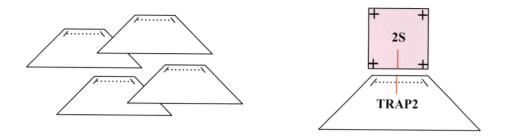

In the same way you marked the beginning, end, and the stitching lines in **Bouquet of Flowers,** mark the stitching lines on wrong side of the shorter parallel edge of TRAP2.

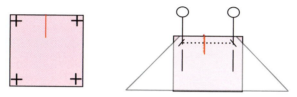

Fold one TRAP2 in half and pinch the center of the short side as shown by the red line. Also fold and pinch the middle of 2S. Instead of drawing them this time, let's try to "eyeball" the corner intersecting points on 2S.

Layer TRAP2 over 2S right sides together matching centers and raw edges. With the wrong side of TRAP2 facing you, insert pins at the ends of the drawn seam line. Continue to insert those same pins into the "eyeballed" 1/4" seam intersections. You'll know you did it right if two tiny bunny ears appear evenly on both sides of the top edge. Sew the seam only on the drawn line. Backstitch at the beginning and end of the seam. These two edges are cut on the straight of grain and should not stretch out of shape. Rotate the sub-unit one half turn and attach another TRAP2 to the opposite side of 2S.

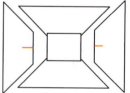

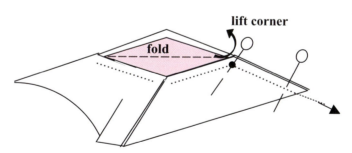

Without catching adjoining TRAP2 patches, attach the last two trapezoids to 2S. You'll get a comical unit that looks like it should be able to fly. All that's left to do is sew those floppy diagonal sides to each other.

Begin by folding 2S diagonally in half—this helps keep flying trapezoid ends away from each other so you don't catch them as you sew. Lift the corner edge of 2S up out of the way, too. Pin and stitch from the inner last needle **holes** to the outside edges. (Yes, holes. As you added each TRAP2 to the square, you ended each line of stitching where the adjoining TRAP2 was attached—same hole—or close.) Don't forget to backstitch as you start sewing this diagonal seam. Rotate the unit a quarter turn, refold 2S, and then sew until all four sides are completed.

Make three more spools. Depending upon your choice of block arrangement, press (or repress) your seams to nest and complete this amusing little block using the hold pin technique to match points.

Homework

Using the patterns and instructions that follow, practice working with polygons by:

- Making one block from the parallelogram grouping.
- Choose and make one diamond block.
- Make one of the trapezoid blocks, or make one of the Challenge blocks.
- <u>Optional</u>: make another Challenge block.
- Make templates for Lesson 6: Circles, Curves, and Arcs.

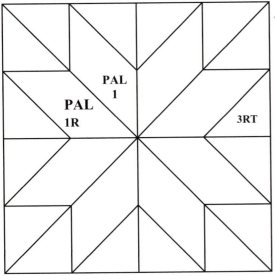

Joined Variable Star

> **Templates:**
> 3RT = Cut 16
> PAL 1&1R = Cut 4 each

About these four blocks: You could make these four-patch blocks using only triangles, as we learned in Lesson 4. Combining shapes into one template eliminates some cutting and sewing. It also creates an opportunity to learn new, sophisticated piecing techniques.

As you cut out the patches for all the variable star derivatives, pay close attention to the grain lines shown on the templates.

Follow the instructions in this lesson to complete the block.

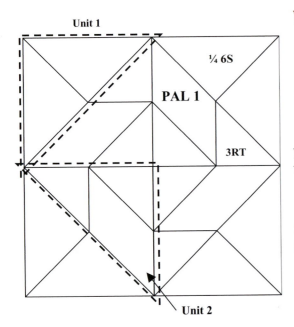

Windblown Square

> **Templates:**
> 3RT = Cut 4
> 1/4 6S = Cut 8
> PAL 1 = Cut 4

About this block: Before cutting PAL 1, be sure your fabric is right side up. The parallelograms in this block face the same direction.

Make Unit 1 by joining two 1/4 6S. To make Unit 2, stitch one 3RT to PAL 1 to make a trapezoid, then attach another 3RT to the shorter parallel side.

> If you use solid color fabrics for the parallelograms, you won't need to worry about right and left-facing templates!

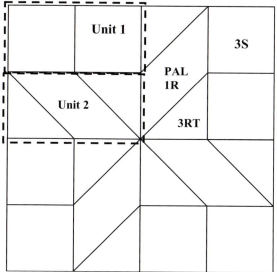

Shooting Star

Templates:
3RT = Cut 8
3S = Cut 8
PAL 1R = Cut 4

About this block: Before cutting, be sure your fabric is wrong side up. These parallelograms are one-way patches.

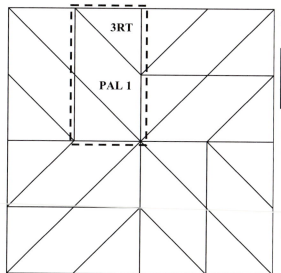

Alsace Lorraine

Templates:
3RT = Cut 16
PAL 1 = Cut 8

About this block: Remember the rule about template orientation on grain line for PAL 1. What side of the fabric should face up for cutting?

There is only one unit in this block. Use floating seams to create opposing seam allowances and press to nest.

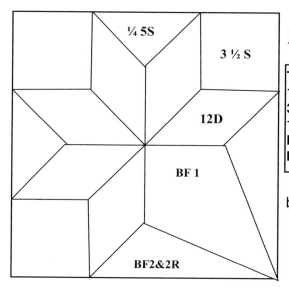

Bouquet of Flowers

Templates:
12D = Cut 6
3-1/2 S = Cut 3
1/4 5S = Cut 2
BF 1 = Cut 1
BF 2&2R = Cut 2

About this block: Instructions for completing this block begin on page 72.

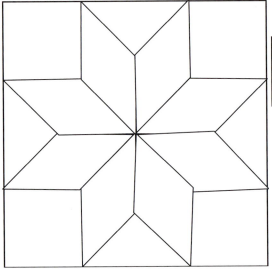

Eight-Pointed Star

Templates:		
12D = Cut 8		
3-1/2 S = Cut 4		
1/4 5S = Cut 4		

About this block: You can do something very exciting and different with this block. You can make it a kaleidoscope, and here's how.

Purchase a sheet of semi-transparent template plastic. Trace 12D onto the plastic with a template marking pencil or indelible pen. Transfer all markings **especially the seam allowance line** and cut it out with paper scissors.

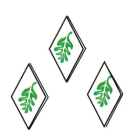

Let's **fussy-cut**! Use one of your fabrics that contains larger design elements such as flowers, paisley, etc. Find an area of the fabric you like that would fit nicely within the 12" diamond. Place your plastic template over that area and trace enough of the design elements so that you can find the same repeat over the surface of your fabric. Now, match up the traced design over the fabric. DRAW the cutting lines, then cut each diamond with scissors, or place your rotary ruler on the lines you drew and use your rotary cutter. I know you have to cut out that diamond eight times, but you'll see it's worth it. Your fabric will look like Swiss cheese, too, but it's still worth it! Sew the diamonds together as instructed for **Bouquet of Flowers** and you'll be amazed at your beautiful kaleidoscope star.

Another instruction about assembling this block: Join two sets of four diamonds only on the seam lines and press seams open. Inset the two squares and one triangle on each half block. You must join the half-blocks together as you did each diamond set – **only on the seam line of the diamonds, not across seam allowances.** You'll actually have a tiny pinhole in the very center because seams did not cross. After the half-blocks are joined, press seams open and inset the side triangles.

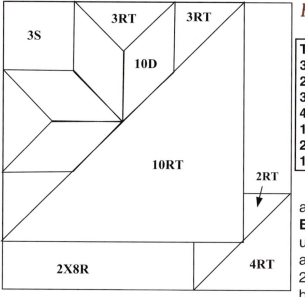

Flower Pot

Templates:		
3S = Cut 1		
2RT = Cut 2		
3RT = Cut 4		
4RT = Cut 1		
10RT = Cut 1		
2X8R = Cut 2		
10D = Cut 4		

About this block: Flower Pot is complex. Its assembly should remind you of **Thistle** or **Bluebell** from Lesson 3. The diamond "flowers" unit 1 and 10RT triangle make a 10" block. By adding background patches 2X8R and 4RT, and 2RT triangles for a base, the 10" flower and pot becomes a 12" block.

Step 1: Make Unit 1 as instructed for **Bouquet of Flowers**. You will only have to set in two triangles and a square. The 3RT triangles on either side of the flower are offset, as you learned with parallelograms.

Step 2: Unit 2 patches are assembled like a log cabin. Attach 2RT to the 2X8R in the proper orientation, then attach each to 10RT. Match centers and sew 4RT to complete the triangle unit.

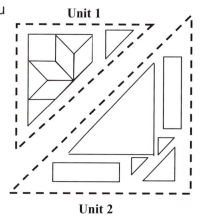

Unit 1

Unit 2

Step 3: Find the Center of 10RT's long side and pin to the exact center of the diamond points. Match corner angles and place a few pins along that outside edge to help control the bias. Join the two units with Unit 1 on top so you can see seam intersections. This time you can sew right across seam allowances being careful to cross one thread above the sewn points.

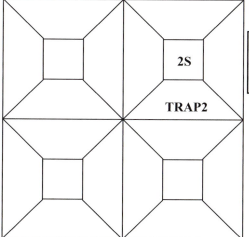

Spools

Templates:	
2S = Cut 4	
TRAP2 = Cut 16	

About this block: The directions for making **Spools** appear in this lesson. As you can see from the tiny illustration above, this block creates the optical illusion of depth. It might be fun to use your fabric colors to make a block of four "tunnels." Just make the top trapezoid dark, the bottom light, the side trapezoids medium, and the center square very light or very dark.

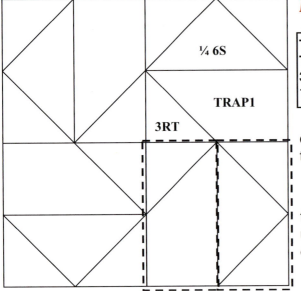

Next-Door Neighbor

Templates:
TRAP 1 = Cut 4
3RT = Cut 12
1/4 6S = Cut 4

About this block: You'll find this block easy to do as long as you press seam allowances toward 3RT to expose matching points.

I suppose you've noticed by now that most four-patch blocks are made up of four identical units that are placed a quarter of a turn from the one next to it.

CHALLENGES

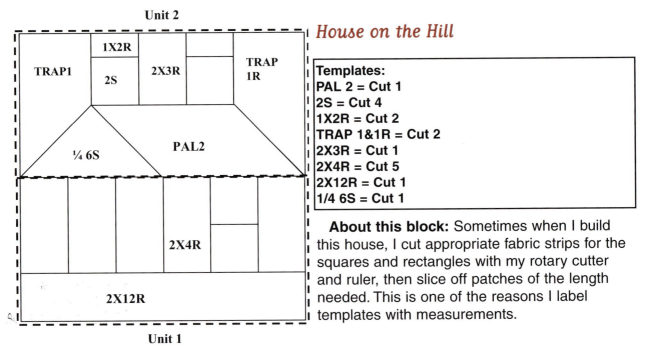

House on the Hill

Templates:
PAL 2 = Cut 1
2S = Cut 4
1X2R = Cut 2
TRAP 1&1R = Cut 2
2X3R = Cut 1
2X4R = Cut 5
2X12R = Cut 1
1/4 6S = Cut 1

About this block: Sometimes when I build this house, I cut appropriate fabric strips for the squares and rectangles with my rotary cutter and ruler, then slice off patches of the length needed. This is one of the reasons I label templates with measurements.

It's fun to choose fabrics that mimic sky, bricks, wood, shingles, and grass. You might even want to add embellishments to this block such as little snips of lace for curtains at the window. You could add a button doorknob and put an embroidered bird in the sky.

Step 1: There's nothing difficult in making Unit 1. You can do it with one hand tied behind your back. If you will be adding fabric embellishments, baste them to the patches before you assemble. Pin anything out of the way that might be caught when sewing seams.

Unit 2 is another matter.

Step 2: You know how to make the chimneys with the "sky" patch in between.

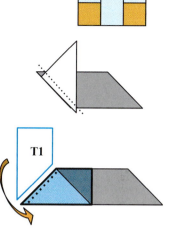

Step 3: You also know how to sew a triangle onto the PAL2 roof.

Step 4: Now it gets confusing. In fact, the first time I taught this block, I showed everyone how to put the TRAP1 sky on *backwards*. If you lay out your patches just like the drawing, it's a simple matter of flipping TRAP1 over right sides together with 1/4 6S. TRAP 1's lines and angles match up with the gable and the roof. Pin and sew the seam from the points to within 1/4" of the roof ridge, and **backstitch 1/4".**

Step 5: This is your lucky opportunity to set in a pieced rectangle! Not only that, you get to set in TRAP1R. Draw your seam lines on the left chimney as shown then set in the pieced rectangle. When you sew the seam joining the "roof ridge" to the pieced rectangle, stop and backstitch 1/4" from the edge. Set in TRAP1R.

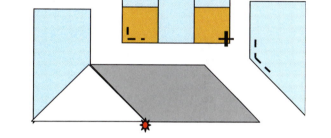

Step 6: Complete **House on the Hill** by sewing Unit 1 to Unit 2. You only have one point to match.

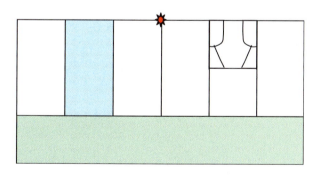

Jacqueline E. Wilson
91 Utica Ave.
Collingswood, NJ 08108

That was hard work, and you did a great job! Bet you didn't know you were a carpenter as well as a quilter!

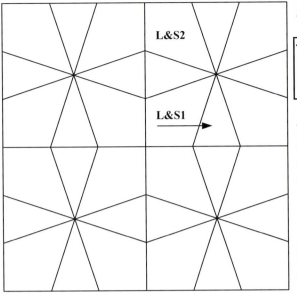

Light and Shadow

Templates:
Light & Shadow 1
Light & Shadow 2

About this block: **Light & Shadow** is a favorite of Amish quiltmakers. It is made in a very different way. You might think of it as an irregular eight-point diamond block with background squares and triangles already attached.

Experiment with different ways of coloring the patches. When blocks are placed edge to edge, the straight lines of the isosceles triangles almost appear curved.

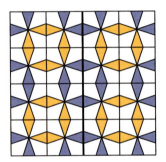

Step 1: Arrange the patches to make one fourth of the block wrong side up. Draw the seam line from the outside edge to within 1/4" of the inside point on the right edge of all patches.

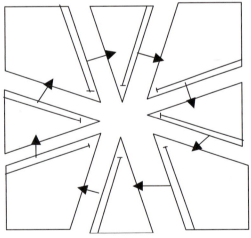

Step 2: Refer to the instructions for sewing a diamond star seam by slightly increasing the seam width at the center. For strength, begin stitching and backstitch 1/4" from the narrow point, then sew to the raw edge.

The unit is put together by sewing one patch to the next, to the next, etc., until you have all eight attached in a series. As you attach each successive piece, place a pin in the seam starting point of the to-be added patch and through the hole that was made by the first stitch in the one you're sewing it to. Stitch the last patch to the first to complete the block. Press the seams open.

Step 3: Make four of these units. To make it easier when you sew them together to finish the block, change some of the open seams to floating seams to allow for nesting.

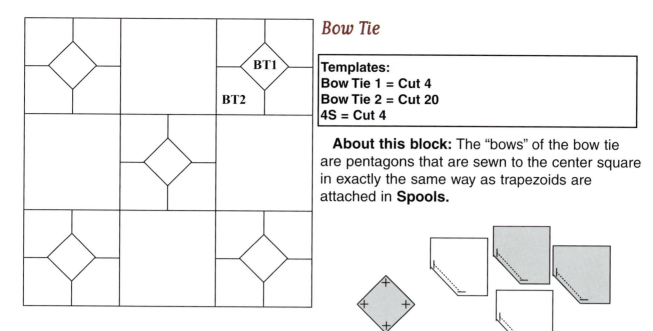

Bow Tie

Templates:
Bow Tie 1 = Cut 4
Bow Tie 2 = Cut 20
4S = Cut 4

About this block: The "bows" of the bow tie are pentagons that are sewn to the center square in exactly the same way as trapezoids are attached in **Spools.**

Step 1: Draw seam lines on the diagonal side of "bow." Indicate 1/4" start-and-stop points.

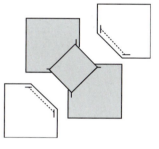

Step 2: With the **Bow Tie 2** on top, sew two identical BT2 to opposite sides of BT1 backstitching at the beginning and ending of the drawn seam line for reinforcement.

Step 3: Finish as instructed for **Spools** in this lesson.

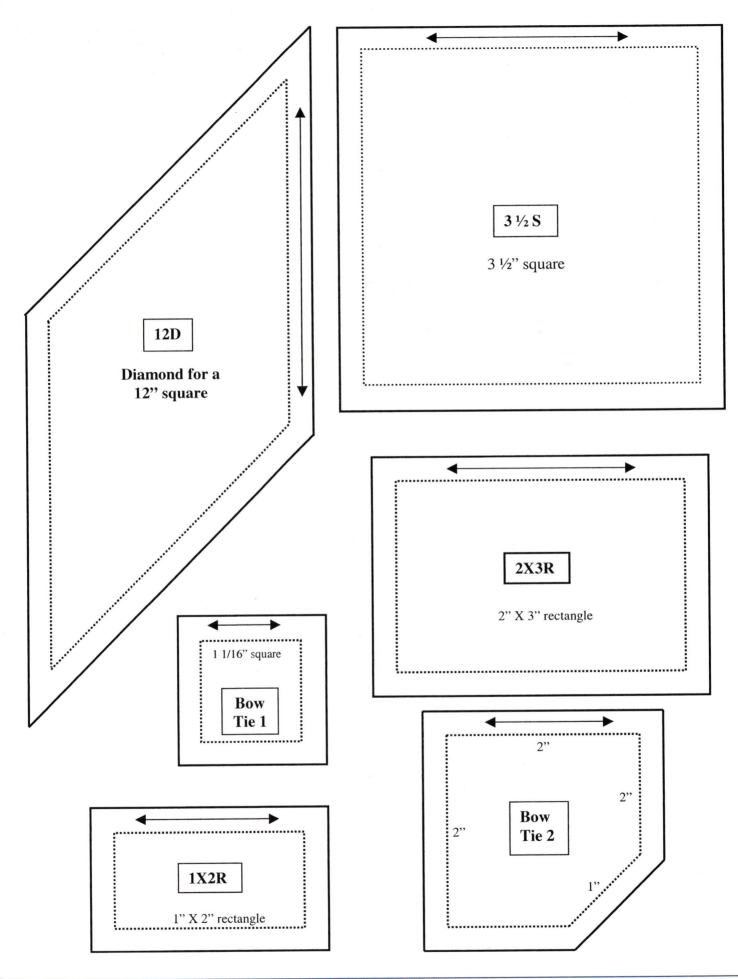

12D

Diamond for a 12" square

3 ½ S

3 ½" square

2X3R

2" X 3" rectangle

1 1/16" square

Bow Tie 1

Bow Tie 2

2"

2"

2"

1"

1X2R

1" X 2" rectangle

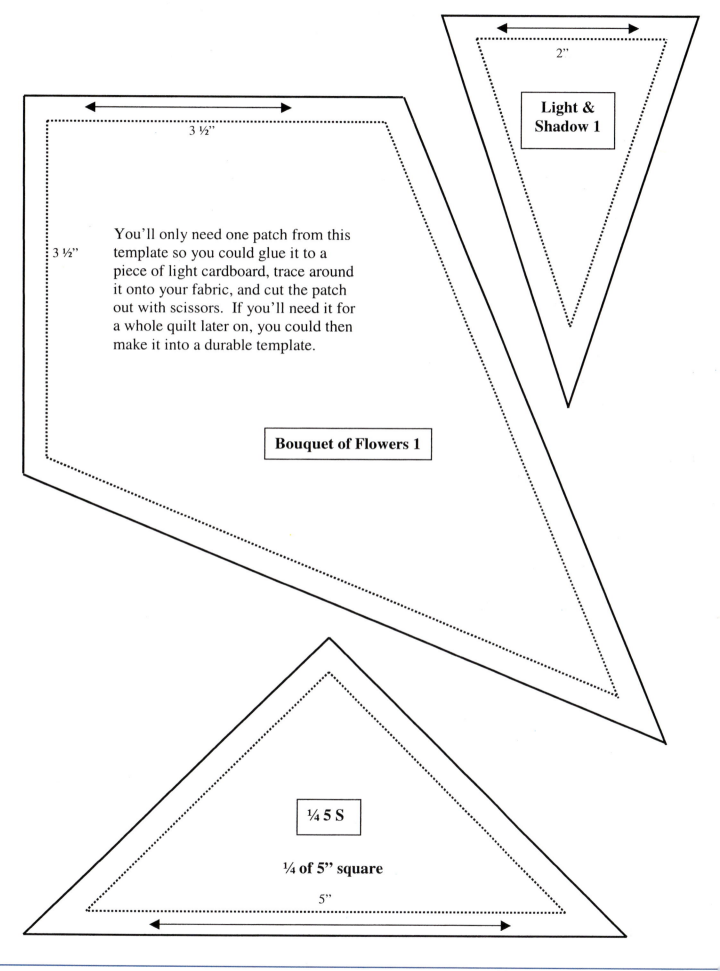

2"

**Light &
Shadow 1**

3 ½"

3 ½"

You'll only need one patch from this
template so you could glue it to a
piece of light cardboard, trace around
it onto your fabric, and cut the patch
out with scissors. If you'll need it for
a whole quilt later on, you could then
make it into a durable template.

Bouquet of Flowers 1

¼ 5 S

¼ of 5" square

5"

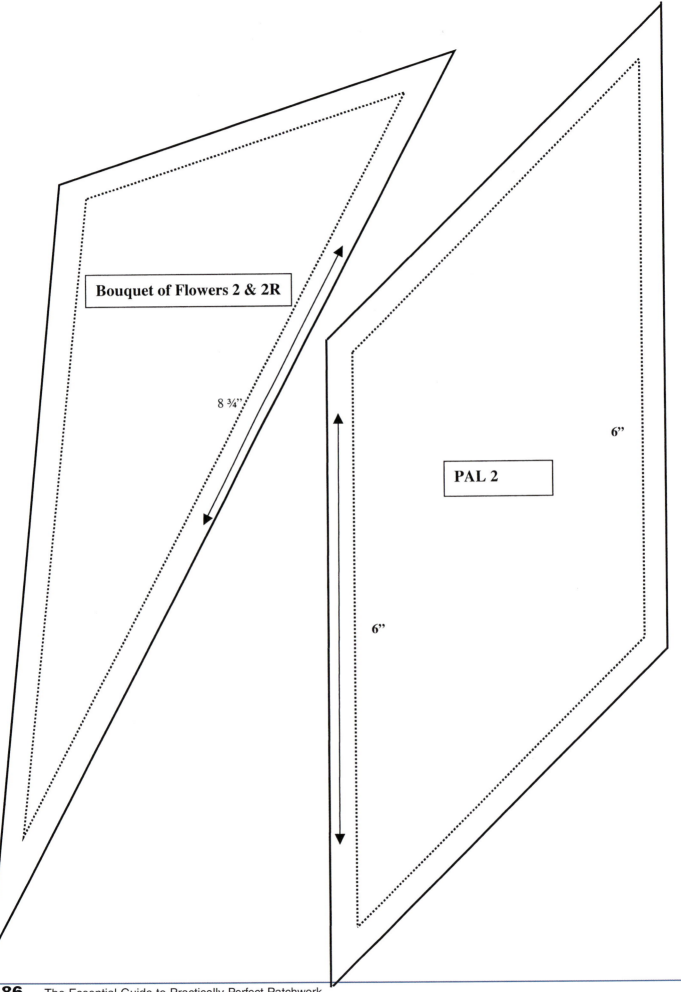

Bouquet of Flowers 2 & 2R

8 ¾"

PAL 2

6"

6"

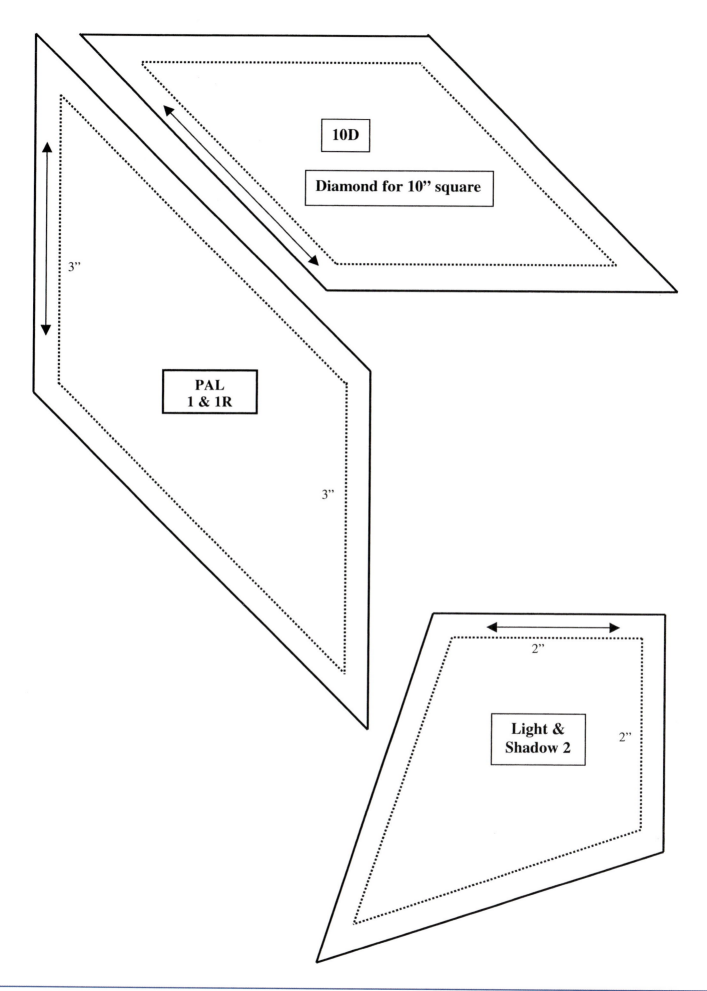

10D

Diamond for 10" square

3"

3"

**PAL
1 & 1R**

2"

**Light &
Shadow 2**

2"

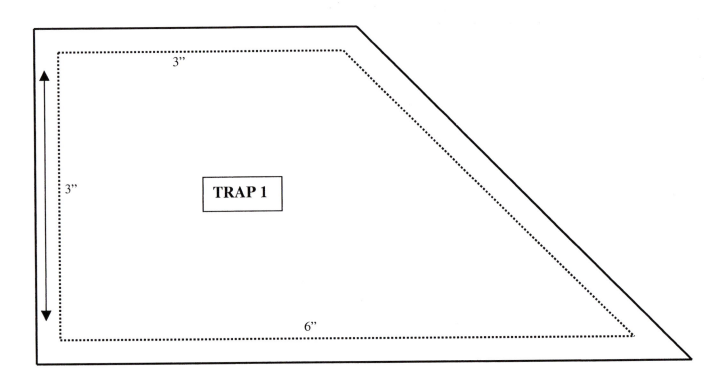

TRAP 1

3"

3"

6"

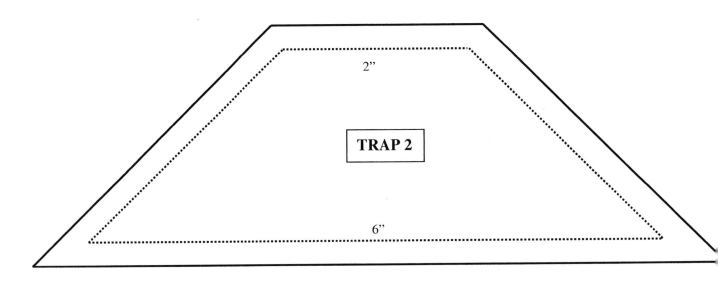

TRAP 2

2"

6"

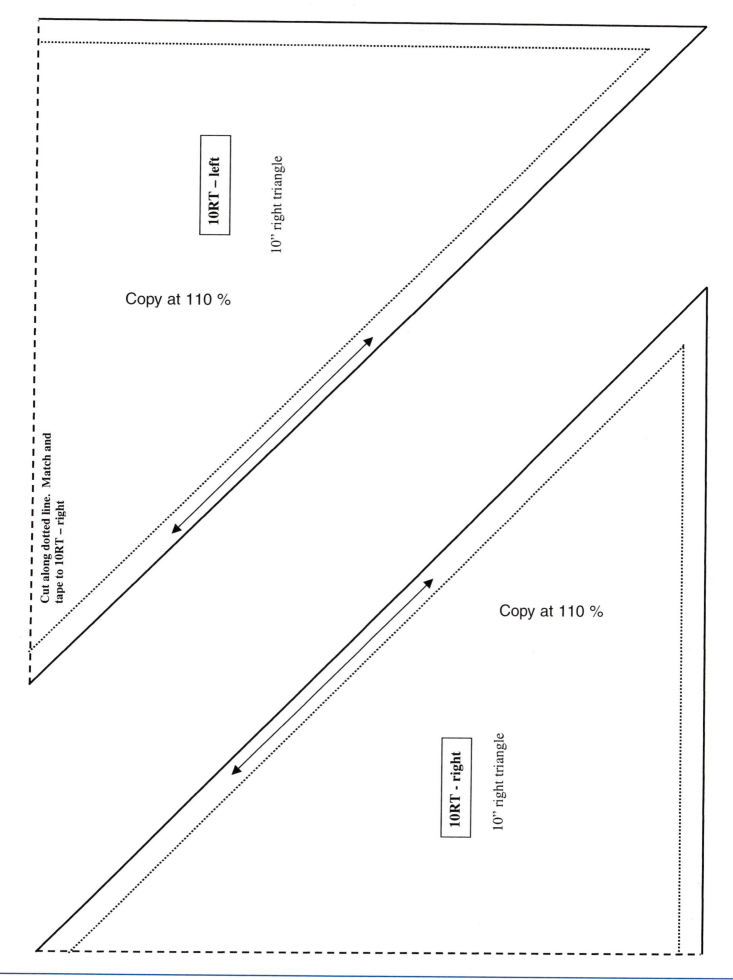

10RT – left

10" right triangle

Copy at 110 %

Cut along dotted line. Match and tape to 10RT – right

10RT - right

10" right triangle

Copy at 110 %

These larger quarter-circles are easy to sew if you remember that concave goes over convex.

Windflower

Baby Buds contains both gradual and tightly-curved patches.

Baby Buds

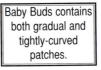

Moon Over the Mountain

Trillium

Around the World

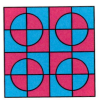

Snowball

Pictures in the Stairwell

Spinning Pinwheel

CHALLENGES
There are so many traditional two-patch curve-in-a- square block designs. Here are four – try making up a few of your own.

Grandmother's Fan

These blocks contain patches with gradual curves and are very stitch-friendly.

Wonder of the World

Drunkard's Path

Circles, Curves, and Arcs

To be truthful, this will be your most difficult sewing lesson. Fabric is woven in straight lines. Machines are manufactured to sew in straight lines. Cutting implements for the most part cut in straight lines. When you go about making straight things into curves, it seems contrary to nature, but it's not impossible. You need to know how to create curved seams if you want to have complete command of all the patchwork skills. There are time-proven methods and techniques to help us sew circles, curves, and arcs, and you will understand how and be able to do it well after you complete your blocks from this lesson.

Concave Versus Convex

What's concave? What's convex? These terms are used to describe the two types of curved patches you will learn to sew together.

This curved patch contains a concave arc. It looks like a "bite" has been taken out of it. An easy way to remember concave is that a cave is an indentation in a rock.

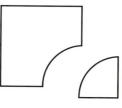

This patch contains a convex curve. It looks like a piece of pie and fills the "bite" taken out of the concave patch.

Negative Templates and "The Bite"

A new cutting method for making two of the concave patches is introduced in this lesson. We've certainly been using our rotary cutters to cut clean, straight lines. Rotary cutters will also make convex cuts. They will even make **easy** concave cuts. They will not make **tight** concave cuts.

For years I made patches containing tight concave curves by cutting straight and convex template lines with a rotary cutter, then drawing the concave curve with a pencil, removing the template, pinning the patches together, and cutting on the drawn curve line with scissors.

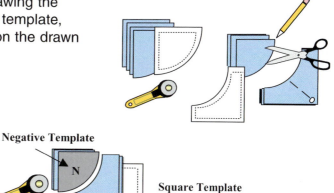

Convex Template

Negative Template

Square Template

Then I thought of using a negative template. I reasoned that every concave cut is really the other side of a convex cut, if only you had the right size template to take the "bite" out of the square.

The convex template that fills the "bite" couldn't be used because it includes seam allowances. You can't cut those off. Negative templates do not include any seam allowances, so they are smaller than the template used to cut the convex patches and take just the right amount of "bite" out of the square.

Negative templates are identified with an "N" preceding the template name/measurements, and tell you what other template to use for whole patches before you take out the "bite." N4X4QC (QC = quarter circle) takes the "bite" out of 6S (from Lesson 3) to cut the large concave patches for **Pictures in the Stairwell**. Negative template N2X2QC takes the bite out of 3S to make the concave patch for **Around the World, Snowball, Wonder of the World**, and **Drunkard's Path**. Both of these negative templates are used for **Baby Buds**.

All you have to do is cut the square as usual. Position the special negative template at one corner of the stack of squares and carefully cut only the curve. *Voila* – there are the concave patches! A paper template is provided with the patterns to compare with your cut patches for accuracy.

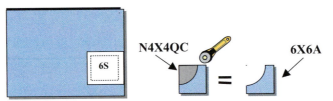

If you're wondering why a negative "bite" template isn't needed to cut the sky background in **Moon Over the Mountain**, it's because the patch is cut on the fold and has a concave curve easily cut with a rotary cutter. **Windflower, Trillium,** and **Pinwheel** also have the same type of gentle arc that can be cut with a rotary cutter.

Cutting Concave Fabric Patches

Just as you had to take special care in cutting those curved template lines, you have to take that same extra care in cutting the curved fabric patches. Only the smaller 28mm rotary cutter is able to perform this task. You could also try the rotary point cutter, a new instrument on the market, which seems to have been made for the job of accurately cutting gently arched concave curves. There are a few guidelines to follow for the use of each tool. With both instruments, always make the concave cut first. Just in case you might have cut the curve too deeply, check to see if you need to reposition the template on the curved cut edge before you make the straight cuts.

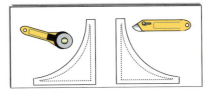

If you are using the rotary cutter, hold it at a comfortable angle and slowly, almost haltingly, cut the fabric, being careful not to cut into the template. If you do nick the template, stop—don't cut a chunk out. Back the cutter out of the slit, and set it back on track. After you have completed cutting the whole patch, you can repair the slit by filling it with white glue. When the glue has dried, you can add a bit of transparent tape to the paper side. You may need to file the edge smooth again.

The new rotary point cutter almost eliminates the chance of accidentally cutting into your cardboard template. A new blade will cut four layers of fabric cleanly, and does do a fine job of cutting those concave curves. Use the tip of the pie-shaped blade and follow the curved edge of the template as you cut. Continue to cut the straight edges of the template with your rotary cutter.

If this is just way too much fooling around for you, do as I used to do: Cut the concave template straight sides with the rotary cutter, draw the concave cut line, remove the template and pin the layers of fabric together, then cut the curve with your scissors.

Basic Curve-in-a-Square Instructions

Even though there are four different configurations of curves, all use the same basic Curve-in-a-Square Principle for assembly, so there's only one new set of sewing instructions to follow to help you make curved seams. (Hooray!)

To stitch a curved seam, remember one basic principal: **Always sew the two patches together with the concave patch on top.** The convex curve does not change its shape when sewn to the concave patch, so it can be placed on the bottom against the feed dogs. You don't have to worry about adjusting it. The concave patch, on the other hand, changes its shape considerably as it is sewn to the convex patch, and you will have to watch for puckering and catching tucks in the seam line. This is contrary to placing the "fussy" fabric against the feed dogs for easing, but placed on top, you can easily see what is happening as you sew the seam.

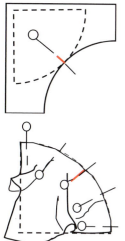

Step 1: Mark the centers of the arcs on both patches by folding each one in half and pinching. Pin the two arcs right sides together at the centers. Make sure the convex patch is on the bottom and right sides are facing each other.

Step 2: Adjust and pin the arc of the concave patch so that raw edges are even and the end corners of the curves are "squared" up to each other. The sides adjacent to the arcs of both patches are straight, so align them and pin. Even though you aligned the beginning and ending of the arc, you may see a slight offset of the patches as your needle enters and exits. This is correct.

Step 3: As you start sewing the 1/4" seam, you will be **clearing the pathway for the needle**. Begin and end the seam with a few backstitches. **Take your time.** Using a stiletto or sharpened chopstick like an extra-long finger helps hold the fabric edges.

Step 4: Leaving the machine needle "down" in the fabric, stop sewing as necessary to see if you have caught any tucks in the concave patch. Make any readjustments and complete the seam. This is kind of a stitch/adjust/stitch effort. Use the last pin as a handle to keep the subunit from skewing sideways as it exits the needle. You'll soon get so good at sewing these curved seams, you'll be able to do them in one fell swoop using only three pins!

Step 5: According to the placement diagram for the block you are making, press all seam allowances to nest for ease of assembly.

This lesson is short and sweet. As I said before, the basic curve-in-a-square instructions hold true for sewing all curved patches together. Larger curved patches, and patches that are gently curved are easier to sew than tighter, smaller curved patches. The easy arc of the patches in **Windflower, Trillium,** and **Spinning Pinwheel** are easier to sew than the tighter curves of **Around the World, Snowball, Wonder of the World,** and **Drunkard's Path**, although the curves in **Around the World** and **Drunkard's Path** don't touch, so you won't have to match many intersections. **Pinwheel** has no seams to match, and a small, appliquéd circle covers the center! What more could you ask? Have fun making these blocks.

Homework

Follow the individual instructions for each block and learn how to sew curved patches.
- Make one block containing a large quarter circle.
- Make one of the "easy" curve blocks in the second column of the color page.
- Make one of the traditional two-patch curve-in-a-square blocks. Each of these five blocks contains 16 subunits. You can see that **Baby Buds** is easiest.
- NO MORE TEMPLATES TO MAKE!

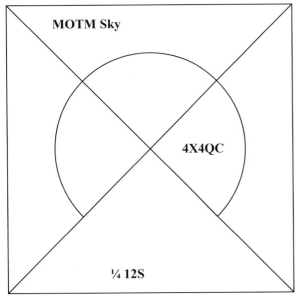

MOTM Sky

4X4QC

¼ 12S

Moon Over the Mountain

Templates:
4X4QC = Cut 3
1/4 12S = Cut 1
MOTM Sky = Cut 3 on fold

About this block: Moon Over the Mountain is such a fun block to make. You can choose fabrics that mimic sky, moon, and grassy mountain.

See basic instructions for joining curved patches.

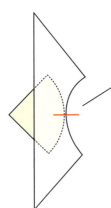

Step 1: Fold and pinch the centers of the arcs on 4X4QC and MOTM Sky. Match centers right sides together placing the concave "sky" over the convex "moon." Pin. Adjust the arc of the sky patch to fit the curve of the moon, square up ends and pin as instructed in this lesson. Carefully stitch seam easing in fullness. Make three. Press the curved seam of two patches to the sky and one to the moon. The sub-unit with the curved seam pressed to the moon will be at the top of the block.

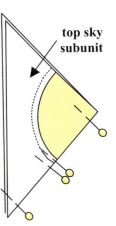

top sky subunit

Step 2: Pin the top sky subunit to the right sky subunit right sides together. Because you pressed the one curved seam allowance in opposition to the other two, the curved seams will nest just like straight seams. Sew from the moon patch to the outside edge using the last pin as a handle. Press the seam in whichever direction makes your unit look the best.

Step 3: Right sides together, join the third sky unit to the left side of the mountain patch. Press the resulting seam in opposition to the two-piece sky unit you just made. You've got two pieced half-square triangles!

Step 4: Pin and stitch your two pieced 12" right triangles together to complete the block. Trim all bunny ears and press the seam towards the darker fabric or whichever way looks best.

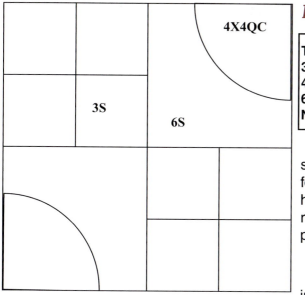

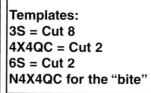

3S

6S

Pictures in the Stairwell

Templates:
3S = Cut 8
4X4QC = Cut 2
6S = Cut 2
N4X4QC for the "bite"

About this block: Pictures in the Stairwell should be quite easy for you to stitch. Two little four-patch units make up half the block. You only have to set in two curved patches to complete the rest. This is a four-patch block made of two four-patch units and two two-patch units.

I know you can make this block by following the instructions you learned in this lesson. Just compare your concave patches with 6X6A. You're already an experienced in making four-patch units, pressing seams to nest and making perfect intersections. You don't need me for this one!

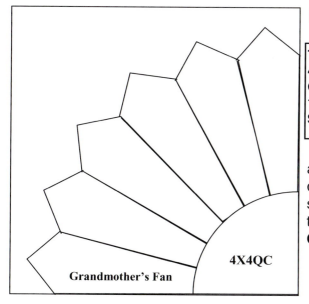

Grandmother's Fan

4X4QC

Grandmother's Fan

Templates:
4X4QC = Cut 1
Grandmother's Fan = Cut 6
12-1/2" X 12 -1/2" Background
Square = Cut 1

About this block: This quaint little block makes a beautiful quilt all by itself and is great for hand quilting and embellishments. The fan blades are sewn together to make a **pieced** concave patch. I think you'll be proud of yourself for making **Grandmother's Fan.**

Take notice of the grainline arrow on the fan blade template. *One* long side of each blade should be on the straight of grain. When you sew the blades to each other, stitch a straight-of-grain edge of one blade to an off-grain edge of the second. This will help keep the fan from stretching out of shape. You will need to plan ahead for color placement before you cut your patches.

Step 1: If you like, cut each fan blade from a different fabric. I know you're wondering how we're going to get that point on the blade. We could just fold and press it under, but chances are the six points would not be uniform. Let's try this little trick:

Fold and lightly press each fan blade in half lengthwise right sides together. Pin, backstitch and sew a 1/4" seam across the wide end from the fold to the raw edge. **Trim** the angle at the fold being careful not to cut into stitching.

Press the seam allowance open.

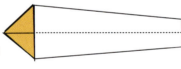

Turn the point right side out. On the wrong side, match the seam line to the center fold of the blade and press the point while pressing away the fold line.

Look at the right side. You have a perfectly shaped fan blade. Make five more.

Step 2: Match two fan blades right sides together and pin. Beginning at the folds of the points, backstitch and join the two patches together on one long side. You don't need to backstitch at the end of the seam line. In this way, join all six fan blades together pressing seam allowances to the darker patch.

Because you planned ahead and sewed a bias side to a straight of grain side, there shouldn't be very much stretching. If there is a little discrepancy at the small ends of the blades, you can trim after all six have been connected, but it won't show because the fan unit will be joined to the quarter circle. You **do** want the "V" where the seam joins the blades to meet perfectly.

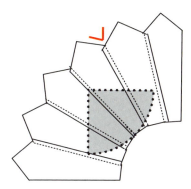

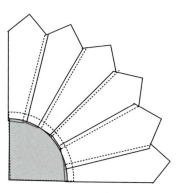

Step 3: Even though the fan unit is pieced, it is now treated as one concave patch. Use the basic curve-in-a square instructions to attach the 4X4QC fan base.

Press the curved seam toward 4X4QC.

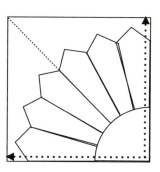

Step 4: We've got the fan but we need to attach it to a background. Cut your background square 12-1/2" X 12-1/2" on the straight of grain using your rotary ruler and cutter. (You might find it easier to cut the square on a fold, in which case you would cut a rectangle that is 6-1/4" X 12-1/2".) Fold the square in half diagonally and lightly press the fold line.

Step 5: Pin the completed fan unit onto the background square aligning the fan center with the diagonal fold and right and bottom edges. Baste the two outside edges together.

Right side of block

Step 6: We need to attach the fan unit to the background square. This attachment is called "applique." For practical quilts, I like to machine applique. The process is speedy and holds patches very securely. Since it's a real bother to keep changing thread colors to topstitch applique, I recommend you use nylon thread. Some nylon threads are difficult to work with and have a mind of their own. I prefer Wonder Invisible® monofilament thread by YLI brand for its strength and compliant characteristics. Choose clear for light colors and smoke for intense or dark colors. You will sew with this thread on the top through the needle. The bobbin thread is the same dressmaker type you have been using for piecing. Later, we'll use this nylon thread when we machine quilt our sampler.

Machine applique is very simple and straight forward. Pin the fan blades flatly and securely to the background fabric. On the right side using the monofilament thread, topstitch each blade point as **close to the edge as possible**. If you see your needle drop off the edge of the fold, **stop** sewing, lift your needle, place it back on track and continue. You'll see that the stitching line is hardly noticeable. Remove the basting stitches at the right and bottom edge of the block.

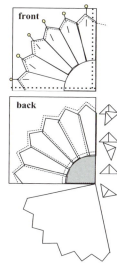

Step 7: Most of my students are afraid to do this next step. Have courage. There is an extra thickness of fabric in your block that you don't need. If you intend to hand quilt your finished sampler, you're not going to appreciate stitching through an extra layer of fabric. The background color you have chosen also may shadow through the fan applique so that the seam allowances will show. We need to cut out the background fabric that is under the applique. We also need to cut off the back folds of the fan blade tips. But we need to cut away these pieces of fabric **leaving a 1/4" seam allowance.**

You do have to be very careful not to cut any part of the fan while leaving 1/4" seam allowances, as shown. You can do it. If not now, maybe just before you assemble your quilt top. A duck-billed applique scissors is perfect for this job, but not absolutely necessary – careful cutting is your best tool.

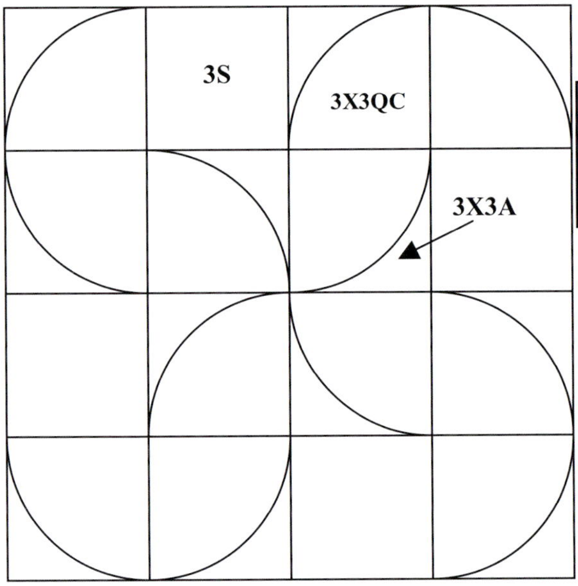

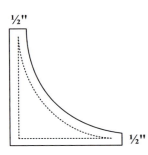

3S

3X3QC

3X3A

Windflower

Templates:
3S = Cut 4
3X3QC = Cut 12
3X3 Easy Arc = Cut 12

About this block: The graceful arcs of these curved patches make such beautiful patchwork blocks and afford limitless design possibilities when creating your own.

See basic instructions for joining curved patches.

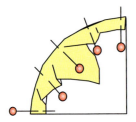

½"

½"

Step 1: Cut the 3X3 Easy Arc patches as described in the lesson for cutting concave curves. There's not much to these patches. The ends of the curve side are quite narrow, and that's good *and* bad. The good part is the patch is very compliant and will stretch easily to conform to 3X3QC. The bad part is they're delicate and could fray, so treat them tenderly. As you can see, the curve ends are only 1/2" wide. That means each end is really two seam allowances. Putting in backstitching at the beginning and ending of the seam line will keep the ends from disintegrating. Make 12 two-patch curve sub-units.

Before assembly, the sub-unit will look something like this. Why, you may ask, is the left pin shown placed in the opposite direction from the others? When I pin the two patches together, I hold them with my left hand, and spread the fullness evenly along the convex curve pinning as I go. First, I pin the centers, then start pinning at the right side of the curve. Because my left thumb is holding the last corner areas of the two patches on the left, I can't let go to put the pin in from right to left. So I put the pin in from left to right. It's a simple matter to remove that pin first after I start the seam.

Step 2: Finish the block as learned in this lesson.

When you match 3S with the pieced two-patch subunit in preparation for joining, you'll automatically be checking the two-patch for correct size.

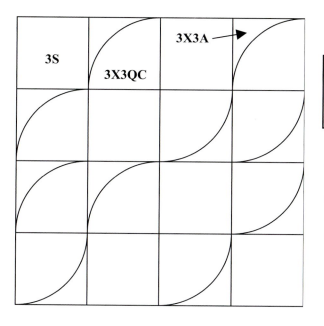

3S

3X3QC

3X3A →

Trillium

Templates:
3S = Cut 6
3X3QC = Cut 10
3X3 Easy Arc = Cut 10

About this block: Spring is so welcome after the long winters of upstate New York where I live. I know the "back of winter is broken" when I see the wild Trillium beginning to bloom. I designed this block to remind me of the promise of spring.

POWER CHECKLIST

√ **Chain piecing**
√ **Use "hold" pin**
√ **Press to nest**
√ **Trim bunny ears**

√ **Match points with imaginative seam allowances**
√ **Creative press for the best look**
√ **Measure completed units for accuracy**

Your Block

Templates:
3S = Cut _____
3X3QC = Cut _____
3X3 Easy Arc = Cut _____

About this block: Try your hand at designing a two-patch curve block. You could cut out 16 paper squares with this easy curve drawn on some or all of them and create a new block by just rearranging them like a puzzle.

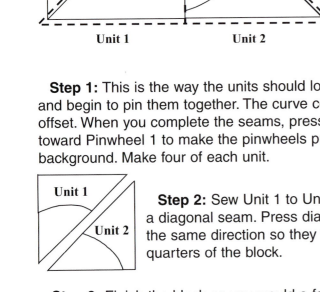

Unit 1   Unit 2

Spinning Pinwheel

Templates:
Spinning Pinwheel 1 = Cut 8
Spinning Pinwheel 2 = Cut 4
Spinning Pinwheel 3 = Cut 4

About this block: I find this old block from the '30s very interesting because the same curved wedge is attached to two differently-shaped background patches. **Spinning Pinwheel** makes a lively scrap quilt with a white background. Follow the basic curve-in-a-square assembly instructions. **Cut all patches with the fabric right side up.** If you use a solid color fabric for the background, be careful not to flip Spinning Pinwheel 2 and 3 over and try to use the wrong side.

Step 1: This is the way the units should look as you match centers and begin to pin them together. The curve corners will show a slight offset. When you complete the seams, press the seam allowance toward Pinwheel 1 to make the pinwheels puff forward from the background. Make four of each unit.

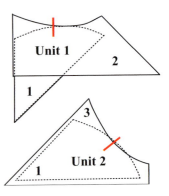

Step 2: Sew Unit 1 to Unit 2 right sides together in a diagonal seam. Press diagonal seam allowances in the same direction so they will nest. Make the four quarters of the block.

Step 3: Finish the block as you would a four-patch.

Step 4: To make the center circle, place a quarter on the wrong side of a scrap of fabric you've chosen for the **Spinning Pinwheel** center. Draw a larger circle around it, as shown. Cut out the fabric circle. With a threaded and knotted needle, sew a running stitch around the outside edge of the fabric circle. Stitch past your starting point. Pull the thread to gather the fabric tight around the quarter. Turn the fabric-covered quarter over, spray starch and press the smooth side with an iron. Loosen the gathers to remove the quarter, draw them up again, knot the thread, and clip. Topstitch the center circle gathered side down onto the block.

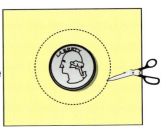

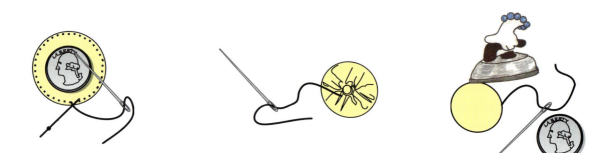

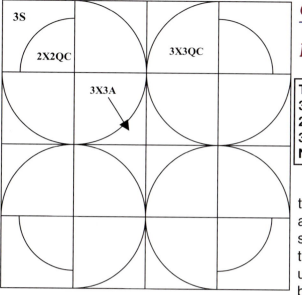

Baby Buds

Templates:
3S = Cut 4
2X2QC = Cut 12
3X3A Easy Arc= Cut 12
N2X2QC for the "bite"

About this block: **Baby Buds** combines both the gentle curved patches found in **Windflower** and **Trillium** with the traditional tight curve-in-a-square patch. Make this block and ease into those challenging little tight curves. You'll get to use the negative template technique to cut four background patches.

Follow the basic curve-in-a-square instructions. Assemble the block in quarters, then join the quarters to complete the block. You might have difficulty meeting the bud outside curves when sewing the quarter blocks together. Just press your seam allowances to nest and use your imaginative seam technique. (See red circle.)

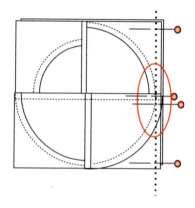

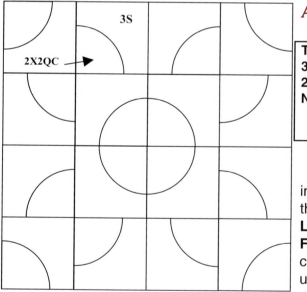

Around the World

Templates:
3S = Cut 16
2X2QC = Cut 16
N2X2QC for the "bite"

About this block: Besides the four presented in this lesson, there must over 30 variations of this 16-unit block. They have names such as **Love Ring**, **Vine of Friendship**, **Nonesuch** and **Fool's Puzzle**. Their only differences are coloration and arrangement of the two-patch sub-units.

Compare your concave patches with 3X3A for accuracy. **Follow the basic curve-in-a-square instructions.** Always refer to your colored diagram while assembling. Press seam allowances for nesting, especially joining the center circle seams. Don't forget to make the block in quarters, then join the quarters to complete the block.

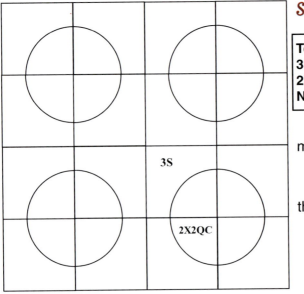

Snowball

Templates:
3S = Cut 16
2X2QC = Cut 16
N2X2QC for the "bite"

About this block: Every seam in **Snowball** makes an intersection!

All four two-patch curve-in-a-square blocks use the same construction techniques.

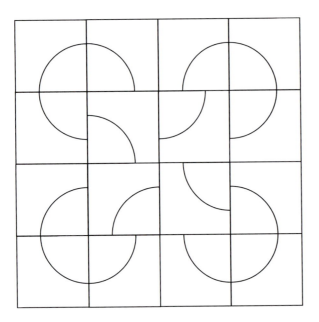

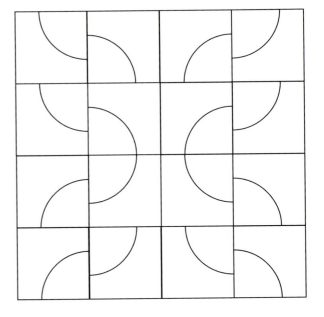

Wonder of the World

Templates:
3S = Cut 16
2X2QC = Cut 16
N2X2QC for the "bite"

Drunkard's Path

Templates:
3S = Cut 16
2X2QC = Cut 16
N2X2QC for the "bite"

Super Skill Booster

It's a little more difficult to make curve and arc templates. They don't have to look beautiful, they just have to be accurate. As you follow Super Bunny's directions, do the best you can. You'll have these templates for a long time. Hopefully, you'll only have to make them once, so be gentle while using them. Remember how precious they were to come by.

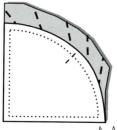

For Quarter-Circle Templates

First, see how well your paper scissors can cut a small piece of scrap cardboard. If it will cut cleanly for about 1/2", you can cut your quarter-circle templates as follows:

After the pattern has been cemented to the cardboard, cut the outside curve of QC and "N" templates with scissors. The scissors won't make that left curve to cut the entire line, so cut as far as you can then shoot off straight, as indicated by the dashed lines in the drawing. Repeat until the curve is cut. Finish the straight lines with the metal ruler and craft knife. Apply the sandpaper layer as usual and trim. Clean up the edges with an emery board.

If your scissors won't cut the cardboard you'll have to cut the convex curves in the same way you will cut the easy concave curves.

For Easy Arc Concave Curves

Hold the red-handled craft knife perpendicular to the cemented cardboard and template. With the very tip of the blade, slowly make the first cut in the concave line of the template. Repeat, increasing pressure with each pass. It becomes easier as the deepening groove you are cutting stabilizes the blade. Take your time. It's the repeats that cut cleanly, more than the pressure. Cut the straight sides with the knife and metal ruler. Attach sandpaper when finished and trim. Clean up edges with emery board.

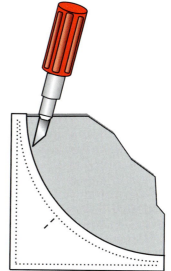

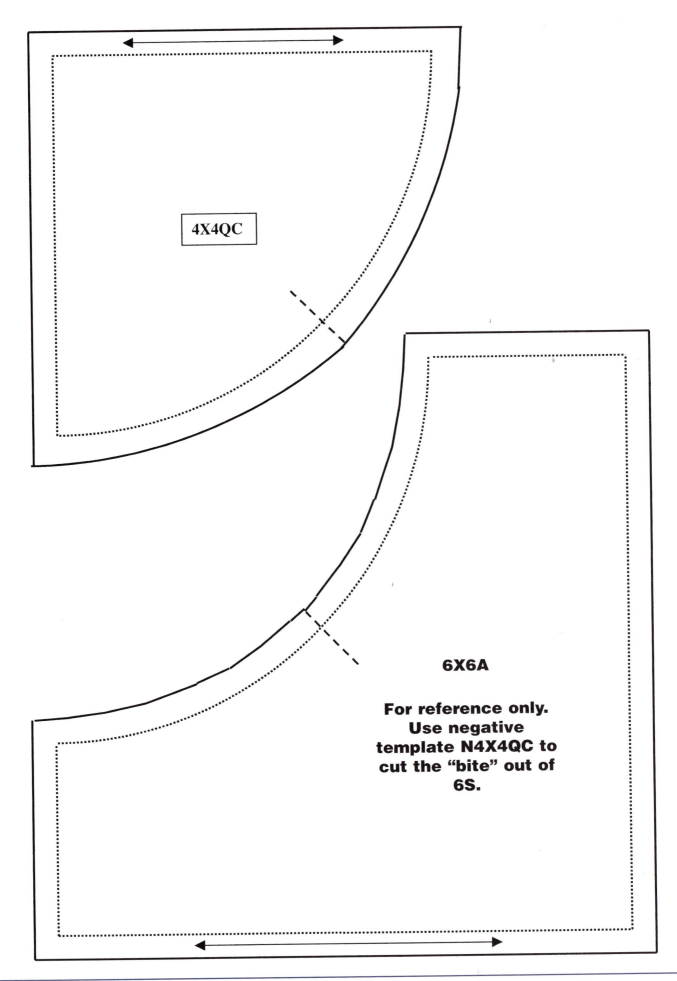

4X4QC

6X6A

**For reference only.
Use negative
template N4X4QC to
cut the "bite" out of
6S.**

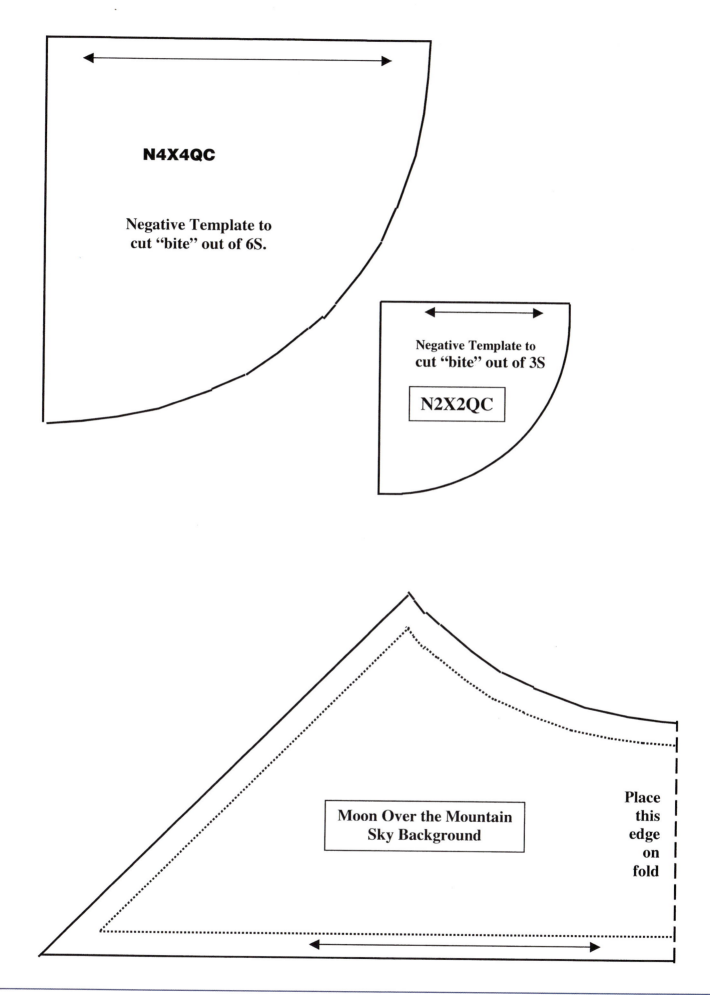

N4X4QC

Negative Template to cut "bite" out of 6S.

Negative Template to cut "bite" out of 3S

N2X2QC

Moon Over the Mountain Sky Background

Place this edge on fold

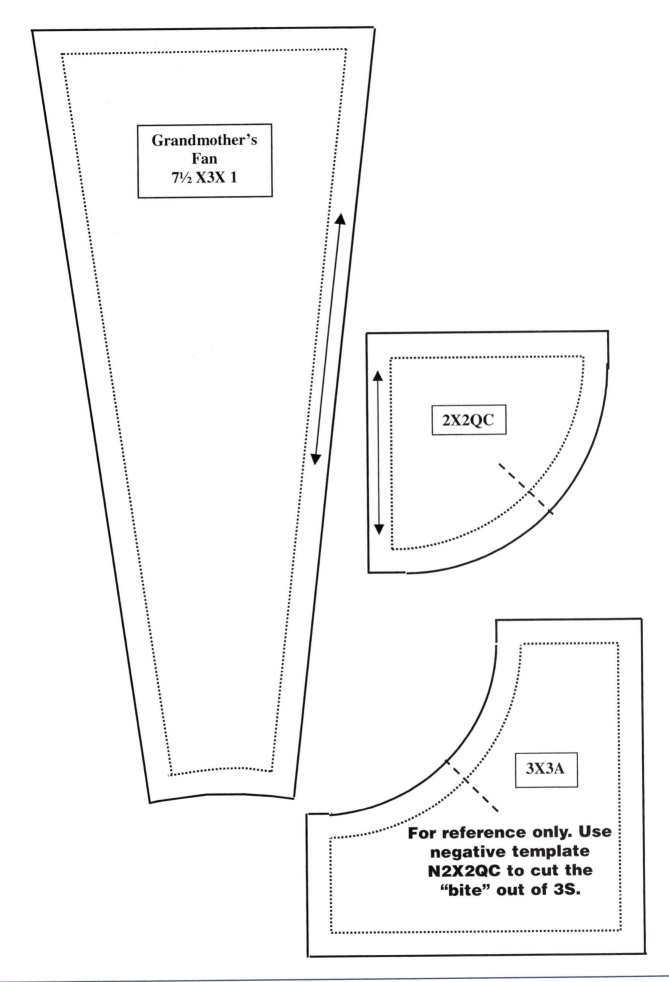

Grandmother's Fan
7½ X3X 1

2X2QC

3X3A

For reference only. Use negative template N2X2QC to cut the "bite" out of 3S.

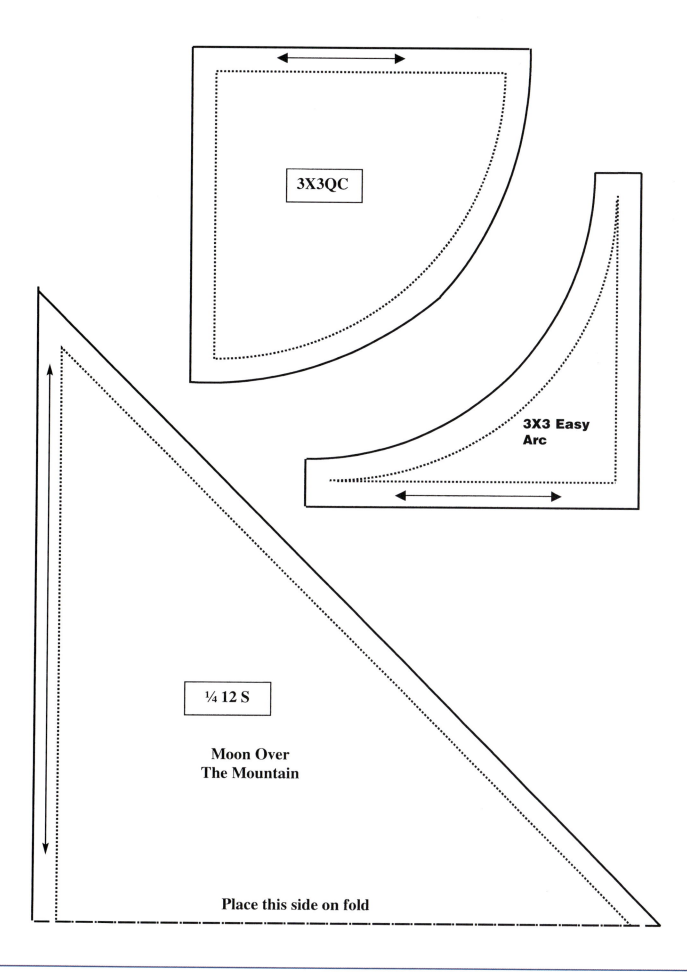

3X3QC

3X3 Easy
Arc

¼ 12 S

Moon Over
The Mountain

Place this side on fold

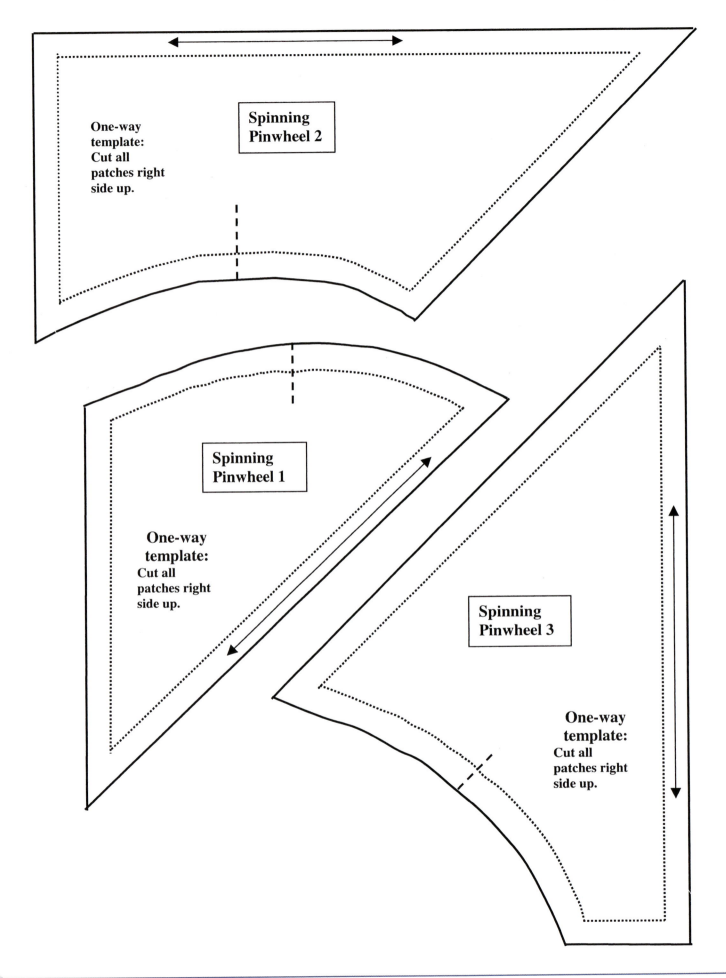

One-way
template:
Cut all
patches right
side up.

Spinning
Pinwheel 2

Spinning
Pinwheel 1

One-way
template:
Cut all
patches right
side up.

Spinning
Pinwheel 3

One-way
template:
Cut all
patches right
side up.

Finishing the Quilt Top
LESSON 7

MATERIALS
Lessons 7 & 8

* Fabric for sashing and borders

* Fabric to make backing that is 6" larger than finished quilt top

* .5 mm mechanical pencil

* Quadrille ruled graph paper

* Rotary grid ruler

* Rotary Cutter and mat

* 15" square rotary grid ruler

* Good fabric scissors

* YLI Wonder Invisible Thread: clear if quilt colors are light; smoke if the colors are bright or dark

* Batting that is 6" larger than finished quilt top

* Size #1 nickel-plated safety pins

* Masking tape

* Large Binder clips (found in office supply stores)

Finishing the Quilt Block

You have reached an exciting moment in the birth of your quilt. The time has arrived to sew all your blocks together and transform them into a quilt top. Quilt blocks sewn together, with or without sashings and/or borders, are referred to as a quilt top. Only after the top is layered over batting and backing, and either stitched or tied together, does it become a quilt. For our example quilt, sashings will be used to join blocks together.

Let's Play "Block Doctor"

No matter how careful you are in constructing your blocks, fabric patches sometimes have a mind of their own and, when assembled, might not "measure up." Often, the sides of our blocks have uneven edges. There are a variety of causes for this, including varying seam allowances, looseness of fabric weave, and patches cut too large or too small. These minor discrepancies can be easily corrected. So, let's "operate" and shape them to the correct size. The goal is to adjust the blocks so that they are within 1/4" of each other, more or less, with sides as straight as possible. Don't get crazy about it. The later addition of sashing will also help adjust size.

Measure each of your finished blocks **across the centers:** top to bottom and side to side. Write down these measurements on a piece of paper. Look at the written dimensions of your blocks. What size are the majority of them? These are **your goal measurements.** While you are measuring, sort your blocks into three piles: too large, too small, and "practically perfect."

If your blocks are approximately 1/8" larger or smaller than your goal measurements, I consider that a home run, and you will not need to fix them.

Here are the measurements for the blocks in the Gold and Black Sampler quilt I made for this book:

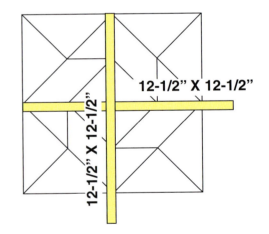

12-1/2" X 12-1/2"

12-1/2" X 12-1/2"

Fan =	12-1/2"	x	12-1/2"
Flower =	12-1/2"	x	12-1/2"
Road to Oklahoma =	12-1/2"	x	12-1/2"
Around the World =	12-1/2"	x	12-1/2"
Bouquet =	12-1/4"	x	12-3/8"
Snowball & 9-Patch =	12-1/2"	x	12-1/2"
Pinwheel =	12-3/4"	x	12-5/8"
Windblown Square =	12-3/8"	x	12-1/2"
Basket =	12-1/2"	x	12-1/2"
Joined Variable Star =	12-1/2"	x	12-5/8"
Spools =	12-1/2"	x	12-1/2"
Spinning Pinwheel =	12-5/8"	x	12-1/2"

Even though I've been sewing patchwork for 30 years, you can see my blocks still don't come out perfectly. You may have a larger difference because, after all, this is one of your first attempts at sewing patchwork. It's reassuring to know that there's something you can do to make your blocks approximately all the same size.

Blocks too Small? This is an easy fix. All you need to do is add a narrow border around all four sides of an undersized block. For example, this **Road to Oklahoma** block is 12-1/8" square and we want to bring it up to our goal size of 12-1/2" x 12-1/2". The block is 3/8" too small on both the width and the length. You can't just add two 3/8" strips to only two sides because it wouldn't look balanced.

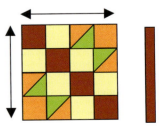

We could make a lot of mathematical calculations here, but basically what we're after is a larger block. We know we'll need to add **half of 3/8" to each side**, include the seam allowances we'll take away from the existing block (1/4" x 2) **plus** add the seam allowances for the fill strips (another 1/4" x 2). I know from experience that narrow strips are hard to apply, so **cut 2" strips** and sew them to all sides just as we learned to add "logs" to the log cabin-type blocks. Then trim the block to the correct size.

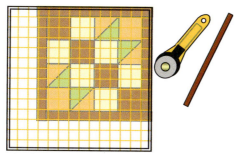

Think about how this "special" block will look in the quilt because the added border will draw attention to it. If you want it to go with the rest of the blocks, make the border out of the least noticeable color that will blend with the block itself.

This square rotary ruler is almost indispensable when "operating" on your blocks. It makes it so easy to "square-up" and trim off the excess. The 15" size is perfect. I know they're expensive, but you'll be grateful for it now and later when we use it to make your quilt "square" while pin-basting the layers

Creative press the border seam allowances after you add each to the block. What does the newly-enlarged block measure across the centers? Correct the top/bottom, then the side/side by subtracting your block size goal number (12-1/2") from the new block measurements, and divide the remainder by 2 (sides). Use your grid ruler and rotary cutter to trim off excess, i.e., **1-5/16"** from each side. Remember, measure twice, and cut once.

Top/Bottom:	Example	Yours
New Measurement =	15 1/8"	
Goal Measurement =	12-1/2"	
Difference =	2 5/8"	
Divided by 2 sides =	1 5/16"	
Cut off top/bottom:	1 5/16"	

Side/Side:	Example	Yours
New Measurement =	15 1/8"	
Goal Measurement =	12-1/2"	
Difference =	2 5/8"	
Divided by 2 sides =	1 5/16"	

Blocks too large? This presents a different problem. If you just cut off the excess, you might cut off the points of patches in the block that you want to touch the sashing strips. Examine each block that is too large. Can you re-sew joining units with a slightly wider seam to bring its' measurements into line? Remember, the amount you stitch into the increased seam allowance will be doubled because you are affecting two layers (patches).

If you can manipulate your too-large blocks to within approximately 1/4" over your target measurements, you will be able to "quilt out" any fullness. That means the fluff of the batting will take up the excess fullness as you quilt.

Blocks have uneven outside edges? When you sew your blocks to the sashing strips, you will pretend that the outside edges are straight. In order to make your points touch, you may have to anticipate where you will be sewing seam intersections, and maneuver the block as you did when assembling patch units using the imaginative seam allowance and holding pin techniques. As long as there is at least 1/8" of block seam allowance beyond the seam line, the seam won't separate. Use a shorter stitch length with these narrow seams. Even though the block seam allowance may be only 1/8", the seam allowance on the sashing strip should remain 1/4".

If you haven't done so already, you will need to draw a sketch or blueprint of the quilt you want to make. This will be your guide. It doesn't have to be fancy. I like to use 4:1 (4 squares equal 1") graph or quadrille paper to make my quilt diagram. It helps me see the exact proportions of the parts of my quilt top. Assign a value to each square on the grid. One square could equal three inches, which fits these blocks well. Therefore, a 12" block would be represented by 16 little grid squares—four across and four down.

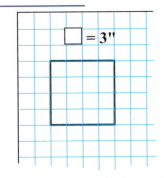

□ = 3"

There are few rules for creating your own top layout, and you have many options. Balance is probably the most important factor. Do you want sashing in between the blocks or no sashing? Sashing separates the blocks so the viewer can appreciate each individual design. Do you want a wide border, a narrow border, or no border? If you choose to add sashing, a width that can be evenly divided into the finished block size looks the best. Usually, if you have sashing, the border should be wider. But I've seen beautiful quilts that break all the rules, and this is your quilt, so follow your instincts.

If you want a large quilt, consider placing your blocks "on-point" and/or adding wider borders or a series of borders. Placed on-point, your quilt's measurements will be based upon the diagonal measurement of your blocks (approximately 17" instead of 12"), and that will make your quilt much larger. Be aware that if you choose the on-point layout, you'll have fill-in triangles that beg for a quilting motif. Look at the examples in Lesson 1 again to help you decide.

A larger quilt means more fabric will be needed for the borders. To cut the borders on the lengthwise grain, which you must do to keep your quilt square, you'll have to buy yardage equivalent to the measurement of your longest border plus at least an additional 1/2 yard.

One of the quilt diagrams shown in Lesson 1 was this on-point setting. Only seven blocks are needed for this wall-hanging size quilt. Ten half-square triangles are used to complete the rectangle. Use the 12RT template for the fill-in triangles included with the stencil patterns at the back of this book

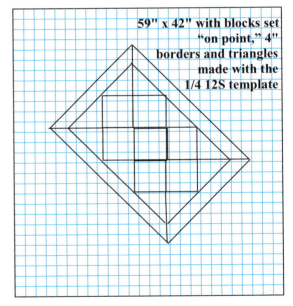

59" x 42" with blocks set "on point," 4" borders and triangles made with the 1/4 12S template

A challenge for the very brave: You can expand on this arrangement and make a bed-size quilt set on-point. A scale drawing is your first step to success. It took me quite some time to realize I had to use the grid lines to draw my blocks, then tilt the paper to draw the outside lines indicating the borders and edges diagonally on the grid.

My choice for the Gold and Black quilt was 3" sashing (which divides evenly into the 12" block size), with a 4" border width (wider than the sashing). I also decided to make little nine-patch blocks at the sashing intersections, expanding on the shortcut method shown in **54-40 or Fight**.

The Gold and Black Sampler will be used as the teaching example for finishing your quilt.

Reserving Border Fabric

I'll bet when you first saw this illustration in Lesson 1, you didn't have a clue what it meant other than you couldn't use most of the fabric you chose for sashing and borders in your quilt blocks. Here comes the best example of using the inherent qualities of fabric to your advantage.

There are good reasons why we use the lengthwise grain for our borders and the crosswise grain for the sashing. Remember that the lengthwise grain does not stretch. The borders will be corralling your quilt top, and no matter what's stretching there, the borders will contain it and make your quilt top square.

Sashing cut on the crosswise grain, on the other hand, will stretch a little, and that's exactly what we need to accommodate the differently sized blocks sewn to the same sashing strip. Isn't that great!

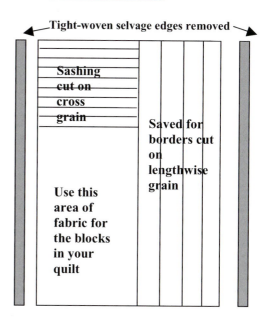

Usable width of fabric is approximately 40"

Before we make either the borders or the sashing strips, we have to get rid of the tightly woven selvage edges. It's difficult to cut them off evenly with scissors or a rotary cutter, but it's a breeze to tear them off "on grain." So make a little snip just past where you can see that the fabric threads are woven closer to each other and rip away! Save those strips and cut them into short lengths. They're great for tying up your tomato plants and long-stemmed flowers. Another thing I like to do in the spring is hang the little strips on tree and bush branches. The birds love to weave them into their nests, and you'll soon see colorful strips of your fabrics in the trees.

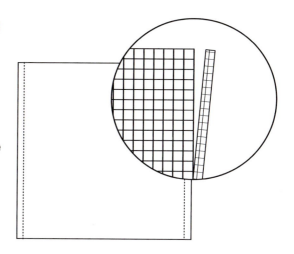

Since we're on a "tear," let's tear off and reserve the border fabric. To make the example quilt, we'll need to save about 20" of lengthwise grain fabric for the borders. Add 2" to make allowance for any mistakes and tear off 22" on the lengthwise grain. (Insert your measurements if your quilt has different dimensions.)

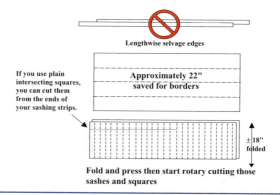

Making the Sashing

I prefer using short individual sashing strips for each block rather than long strips that run either from the top to the bottom or side-to-side. The reason is that it's very difficult to attach two blocks exactly across from each other on one long sashing strip, especially blocks that may not be the same exact size. Improper alignment can make you disappointed in that quilt you worked so hard on.

Use your hand-drawn diagram as a guide to determine how many sashing strips you will need. The width of those strips is your choice, but the length of the strips will be determined by your length/width block goal measurement; for example, if your "doctored" blocks share common measurements of approximately 12-1/2" x 12-1/2", then your sashing strips will be 12-1/2" long.

If you choose plain sashing strips and intersection squares, you may want to omit the perimeter sashes and squares, and attach the borders directly to your blocks—especially if they will be made from the same fabric. You won't notice those other seams, so why make them? Save work wherever you can.

This particular quilt diagram contains sashing strips that are 3" wide. You have reserved 22" on the lengthwise grain for 4" **borders** and have at least another 18" to use for sashing strips. You can get one sashing strip and one corner square out of each length. Use your rotary cutter and mat to cut the number of sashing strips (17) and intersecting squares (6) you will need from the crosswise grain of your folded fabric.

Do You Want to Make Pieced Sashing and Intersection Squares?

Don't let this step intimidate you. To make the Gold and Black quilt layout, you will have to make 31 pieced strips and 20 nine-patch intersection squares. You can use the quick assembly tricks you learned in **54-40 or Fight** to make two different sets, and then cut strips from those sets for squares and sashes.

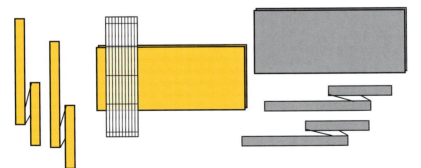

To begin, cut 1-1/2" strips from two fabrics and prepare Sets 1 and 2, from which you will cut the sashing and the nine-patch intersections, also known as "cornerstones."

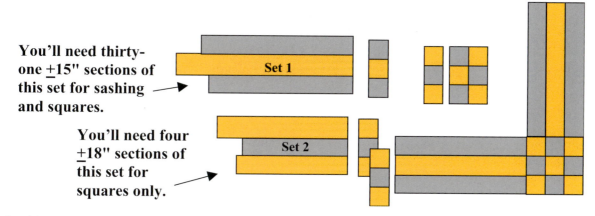

You'll need thirty-one ±15" sections of this set for sashing and squares.

Set 1

You'll need four ±18" sections of this set for squares only.

Set 2

Sashing strips and setting squares have to nest too, so press seam allowances to the darker color, and nesting will be automatic. Don't attach the squares to the strips yet.

How Does Your Quilt Top Look So Far?

Once all the sashing strips are cut and pieced (if necessary), **sew one strip to the bottom of each of your quilt blocks.** You'll get a better idea of how the blocks will look in final form attached to their sashes. Stitch with the wrong side of the blocks on top. Use the same tricks and techniques to meet points and match seam intersections as you did when constructing the blocks. Make the blocks fit the strips.

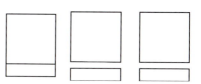

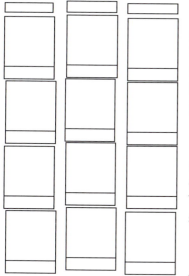

This next step is kind of fun. Lay your blocks out on a large surface and rearrange them to achieve a pleasing combination. Try to balance color and block busy-ness. Some of your blocks might not look that great with all the others. That's why I recommended you make a few extra ones. Turn the orphans into pillows and gifts.

When you find the arrangement you like, sew a sash to the top of each block in the first row. Assemble your quilt top in uneven quarter sections as shown. Don't assemble it in strips. That could lead to "wavy" seams.

Your quilt top is almost finished. Sit back and admire it!

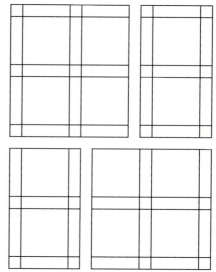

Borders: Does Your Quilt Really Need Them?

A border is to a quilt what a frame is to a painting. Some paintings are so full of color and design that an overly ornate frame would detract from its beauty. Some paintings are too small for the wall, so the addition of a wide frame would nicely fill the space. Some paintings need no frame at all. And some frames are of such beautiful design that they meld with a painting and both complement each other.

Borders can help you achieve these same effects. If your quilt is bright, colorful, and busy, all you would need for a border would be a simple frame of fabric that controls the interior action within a boundary. (What a surprise if a bit of that interior action might escape and fall into the border with the interjection of a small, matching pieced block!) Perhaps you have a quilt top that makes such a strong statement, a border would be superfluous. All that would be necessary to finish this quilt would be a narrow binding. If your quilt top is too small to cover a bed, the addition of a border or number of borders will bring it up to the correct size. Borders are limited only by your imagination—and how much fabric you have left!

> Speaking of leftovers, save pieces of your quilt fabrics.
> You never know when you'll need a repair patch.

Measuring for Borders with Mitered Corners

Well-executed, mitered borders amaze quilt admirers and judges alike, and it isn't that difficult to accomplish. This treatment really does give your quilt a frame. Beauty aside, we must never forget that borders fulfill many practical requirements, not the least of which is to keep our quilt square.

To construct our border, we need to know the top's correct measurements. How do you measure your quilt top? Remember when we measured our individual blocks—we didn't hold the tape along one side, we measured across the centers. Spooky things can happen at the outside edges of our quilt, but its true dimensions are always found right across the middles.

Your quilt measures
_____ **inches top to bottom**
_____ **inches side to side**

Find the correct size to cut your border strips for mitering by using this formula:

How wide will your border be?   _____ **inches.**

For length of top and bottom border strips:

Side to Side measurement =   _____ **inches**
   Plus border width x 2 =   + _____ **inches**
   Add 3" (seam allowances and safety margin)   + 3 **inches**
   Length of top and bottom border strips   _____ **inches**

For length of side border strips:

Top/bottom measurement =   _____ **inches**
   Plus border width x 2 =   + _____ **inches**
   Add 3" (seam allowances and safety margin)   + 3 **inches**
   Length of side border strips   _____ **inches**

To see how this formula works, let's insert the measurements from the example quilt.

Gold and Black top measures _____64_____ " top to bottom
                           _____49_____ " side to side

To find the correct length to cut border strips for mitering, use this formula:
How wide will your border be? _____4_____ "

For top and bottom border strips:
Side measurement = __49__ " plus width of 2 borders = __8__ " plus 3" extra = __60__ "

For side border strips:
Top/bottom measure = __64__ " plus width of 2 borders = __8__ " plus 3" extra = __75__ "

Don't forget to add 1/2" for seam allowances to your border width when cutting. These borders should be cut 4-1/2" wide.

Using your calculated measurements, cut or tear border strips for your quilt top from the lengthwise grain. Tearing will ensure on-grain strips. The torn edges will be a little raggedy and the fabric print could be slightly distorted, but true straight of grain borders are what we're after.

NOTE: If you are planning to add a series of borders around your quilt, tear the strips from the fabrics you will be using. Sew them together then treat each pieced border as one complete unit.

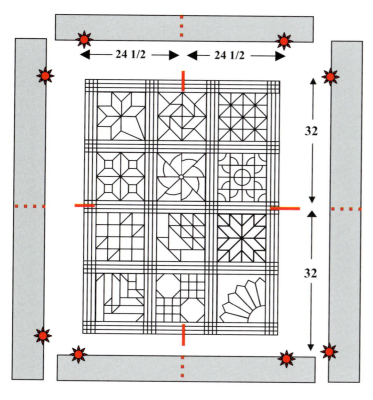

24 1/2 — 24 1/2
32
32

Attaching the Borders

Find the centers of each side of your quilt and mark with a pin. Fold each border strip in half and mark the centers.

We always use the across-center measurements for the size of our quilt. The side-to-side measurement is 49". To attach the top and bottom border strips, calculate half the side-to-side measurement, 24-1/2", then measure 24-1/2" from the center of the top border to each end and mark. Repeat for the bottom strip.

Half the top-to-bottom measurement of 64" is 32". Measure from the center of the side strips and place a mark at the 32" point at each end. Repeat for the other side.

If you are sewing the border right to the blocks with no perimeter sashing strips, use the point matching and creative seam allowance techniques you have learned.

With the wrong side of the quilt facing up, match one side center mark to the center of its border and pin. Align the outside corners of that side of the quilt top to the 32" mark on the border and pin. Ease in fullness and pin the side as necessary. Sew the seam **starting and stopping 1/4" in from the outside edge of the quilt top and backstitch at both seam ends**. Repeat on all four sides. Press the seam allowances toward the borders. Doesn't the quilt with its detached border corners now resemble a large version of a **Spools** unit?

You have just corralled your quilt and it will be square because you used the across-the-middle measurements. Congratulations!

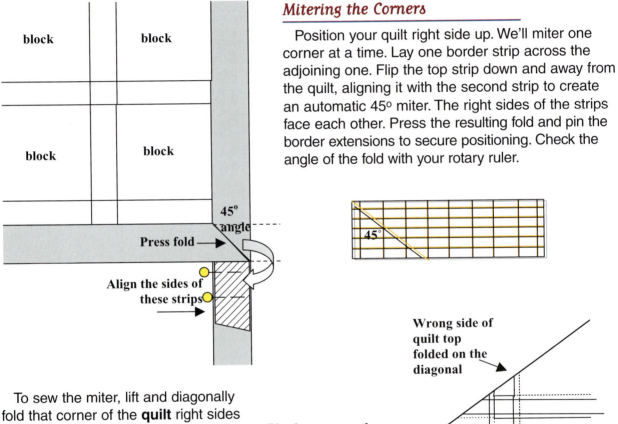

Mitering the Corners

Position your quilt right side up. We'll miter one corner at a time. Lay one border strip across the adjoining one. Flip the top strip down and away from the quilt, aligning it with the second strip to create an automatic 45° miter. The right sides of the strips face each other. Press the resulting fold and pin the border extensions to secure positioning. Check the angle of the fold with your rotary ruler.

To sew the miter, lift and diagonally fold that corner of the **quilt** right sides together matching the outer long border edges. Secure with additional pins. When you sewed the border onto the quilt, you stopped stitching 1/4" from the top's outer corners. Begin stitching the border miter seam in the last stitch holes, backstitch, then follow the pressed fold line, and finish the seam at the raw edge.

Open the quilt and look at the right side of the miter you just made. Again, use the 45-degree line on your rotary ruler to check for accuracy and a square border corner. If it needs no correction, return the quilt to the wrong side and trim excess seam allowance to 1/4". Press the seam open.

Don't Want Mitered Corners?

You can make borders with square corners by cutting squares the width of your border plus 1/2" for seam allowances. (If your borders are 4" wide, the square would be 4-1/2" x 4-1/2".) The top and bottom border strips must be cut to your exact crosswise quilt measurements plus 1/2" for seam allowances. The side borders must be cut your exact lengthwise quilt measurement. Add the squares to the top and bottom borders first. Sew the side borders to the quilt then add the joined top and bottom borders nesting seam intersections.

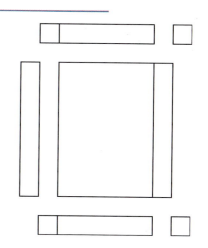

Always make the outer edge of the quilt fit the borders to make your quilt square.

You can also make plain borders. To do this, begin with one across-the-center measurement. (You save fabric if you add the long sides first.) Cut the side borders and add them to the quilt. Measure your quilt again from side-to-side including the new side borders. Cut your top and bottom borders using that measurement, and add them to your quilt so as to make the quilt fit the borders.

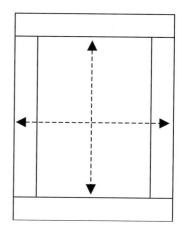

Your Quilt Top is Done!

Give your beautiful **completed** quilt top a good steam pressing. You can use starch or sizing, too. Take final center measurements in preparation for the next lesson, The Three B's—Backing, Batting, and Basting.

Your finished quilt top is _____" long and _____" wide.

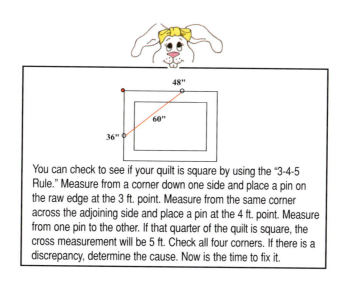

You can check to see if your quilt is square by using the "3-4-5 Rule." Measure from a corner down one side and place a pin on the raw edge at the 3 ft. point. Measure from the same corner across the adjoining side and place a pin at the 4 ft. point. Measure from one pin to the other. If that quarter of the quilt is square, the cross measurement will be 5 ft. Check all four corners. If there is a discrepancy, determine the cause. Now is the time to fix it.

The Three "B's" — Backing, Batting, and Basting
LESSON 8

Backing, Batting, and Basting

This lesson will teach you how to make your quilt into a "sandwich" in preparation to be quilted. Because a quilt is made up of three layers—the top, the batting in the middle, and the backing—we need to make choices on the best types of batting and backing material to purchase for the kind of finish we want to give our quilts.

Choosing a Fabric for the Backing

The fabric you choose for your quilt's backing should be of the same fiber content and quality as the fabrics you used in your quilt top, and that would preferably be a good 100 percent cotton. Don't be tempted to use a cotton sheet just because it's large enough to make a backing with no seams. Some sheets can be very tightly woven and impossible to quilt through. Many contain a mix of cotton and polyester that, with wear, will form little "pills" of fiber on its surface. Some 100 percent cotton sheets are too soft and stretchy for use as a backing.

You can find a few 90"-wide fabrics available, although color and pattern choices are limited. Most quilters choose a 45" cotton fabric that goes well with their top, and piece it to accommodate the quilt's measurements. Janet Yantch, one of my students, took all the larger leftover fabric scraps from her quilt top, pieced them together, and made a backing of simple patchwork squares and rectangles. It was quite wonderful, and her skill in keeping all the backing seam lines straight and perpendicular with the edges of the quilt top was very evident.

What color fabric should you pick for your quilt back? If you want to hand quilt your entire quilt, you should use a light, solid color. Only a plain cotton fabric will reveal the stitching and shadows created by your hand quilting. If you're going to go to all the trouble of hand quilting, you want your hard work to show on the back as well as the front.

Our beginner quilt will contain some hand quilting. It will also be machine quilted in keeping with my philosophy of **"machine quilt where it doesn't show and hand quilt where it does."** In this way, people who look at your quilt will think it is completely hand quilted. But simple machine quilting in the ditch will hurry the chore along so that you will be able to finish your quilt in a relatively short time. Finishing a quilt encourages all of us, especially beginners, to continue making more quilts instead of being hung up on hand quilting for months at a time.

Although the next lesson will concentrate on the actual quilting processes, we have to keep in mind what specific techniques we plan to use in order to purchase the correct backing fabric and quilt batting.

Since this could be your first experience with any type of quilting at all, I suspect your stitch might not be perfection. Mine certainly wasn't when I began quilting—far from it! So let's buy backing fabric that disguises our learning experience. A non-directional, busy print fabric is great for this. Choose a color that blends well with the fabrics you used in your top. It's really great if you can find one that has its design printed in the color of the hand quilting thread you plan to use. This combination is the best camouflage.

Examples of backing fabric

How Much Backing Fabric To Buy

The backing for a quilt should be at least 6" larger (after pre-shrinking) than your quilt top. Why? When you quilt, the top and backing will get smaller as its surfaces are taken up slightly by the stitching and batting. If we made the backing the same size as the top, at the end of the quilting process, the backing could be smaller than the top. We don't want to have to cut the top down to fit the backing. It's better to cut the backing down to fit the top.

In Lesson 7, you measured your completed quilt top after adding the borders. What were your measurements? The finished Gold and Black Sampler top measured 57-1/2" wide by 72-1/2" long. The cotton fabric I wanted to use was 45" wide. (Me, thinking: "So, the quilt is 72-1/2" long—that's a smidge over 2 yards. Twice 2 yards is 4 yards plus the additional 6" [3" x 2 edges] **for each length of fabric**, 12"—that's 1/3 yard more.") I needed 4-1/3 yards, so I bought 4-1/2 yards. It's better to have more than you need than not enough.

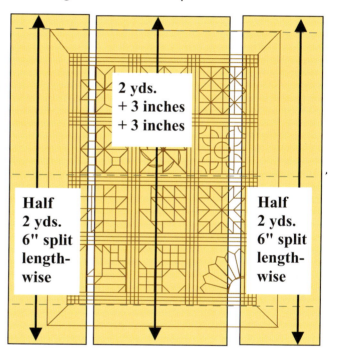

2 yds.
+ 3 inches
+ 3 inches

Half
2 yds.
6" split
length-
wise

Half
2 yds.
6" split
length-
wise

You might wonder why you wouldn't just sew two lengths of fabric with one seam down the middle. You could do that, but a middle seam will carry the weight of the entire quilt as it would lie on a bed. Even though there's batting between the back and top, after time, a wear line tracing the center backing seam could appear on the top. By supporting the weight of the quilt between two backing seams, a wear line is less likely.

Choosing the Batting — Match Fiber Content to Quilting Method

The most readily available quilt batts contain fibers that are all cotton, all polyester, or a combination of polyester and cotton. For practical purposes, I'll omit silk, wool, and down as choices because of expense, accessibility, and/or potential allergy problems. Let's take a moment to discuss the attributes of cotton versus polyester.

Cotton Quilt Batting

Batting made of cotton, a natural fiber, captures less air and is generally less voluminous than polyester. It will not separate if you follow the manufacturer's instructions for quilting distances. Its' fibers will not migrate through the top or backing fabric. Cotton batting gives your quilt a flatter, more traditional look. **The thicker and more dense the cotton batting, the more difficult it is to hand quilt.** Machine quilting through this type of batt looks beautiful, provides the feed dogs with something sturdy to grip onto as it sews, and gives the quilt a substantial and warm look. You will get a good "relief" of shadow and stitch with a dense, cotton batting, but the quilt will be heavier. If I am going to completely machine quilt, I prefer this type of batting for even-stitch results.

Cotton battings come in white or natural (cream) colors. Thick or thin, many are chemically glazed, heat treated, or manufactured so that you can space your quilting up to 8"-10" apart with no danger of bunching or separation. Some brands contain broken seed particles, and the manufacturer recommends that you wash it before use to eliminate the possibility of released oils staining your quilt top. Other brands of cotton batting have been manufactured with the same non-bunching features and do not contain seed particles.

Read the manufacturers' package directions before use. Be especially mindful of how much the cotton quilt batting is expected to shrink. If you want a traditional look for your quilt, a minor amount of shrinkage is desirable and will contribute to the shadowing and "relief" texturing effect.

Polyester Quilt Batting

Polyester, a synthetic fiber, has its attributes, too. It dries faster, retains its volume after washings, does not mildew, won't shrink, and helps keep your quilt from looking wrinkled. Polyester traps more air, thus making your quilt warmer with less weight. You don't have to pre-wash polyester, although you might want to toss the batt into the dryer on low for a few minutes just before you baste it into your quilt to remove the wrinkles caused by packaging.

If you plan to hand quilt, it is much easier to stitch through a 100 percent polyester batt. This characteristic is referred to as "needling quality." Leave the "high," "ultra," and "extra" loft batts for tied quilts. These thicker polyester batts puff up and hide hand quilting. If it's not going to be seen, why do it? Tying a puffy quilt with embroidery floss, heavy cotton thread, yarn or narrow (1/8") ribbon is a perfectly acceptable form of attaching the three layers of a quilt together, and its effective use can become part of the total design of your quilt top.

Polyester battings are also manufactured with surfaces that are heat bonded or treated with a finish that holds their fibers in place. This treatment, too, is intended to prevent bunching, and inhibit the migration of fibers through your quilt fabric and cause what is referred to as "bearding." Inexpensive polyester batting with no surface treatment can ruin a quilt. Minute fibers will continually work their way through the fabric weave and give an unsatisfactory "fuzzy" look. You'll never be able to get those fibers off because brushing, using a "de-fuzzer," or one of those tape garment rolls will just pull more fibers to the surface.

The bearding won't be as noticeable if you use a white batting on a mostly white or light quilt, but will be quite noticeable when used under darker or more intense colors. There are charcoal-colored polyester batts available which make it more difficult to see the "bearding" on these darker quilts, and I highly recommend their use if you want to entirely hand quilt one. Be aware, though, that the dark batting will shadow through and affect the color of any light patches in your quilt.

Glazed or bonded, whatever stabilizing treatment is given to the surface, if you're going to use a polyester batt, the small additional expense is worth paying when you consider how much time and work you will put into making your beautiful quilt.

Cotton-Polyester Blend

Almost all major batting manufacturers have produced a hybrid batt that contains both cotton and polyester fibers. The ratio is cotton in the 80 percent range with around 20 percent polyester and will give your quilt the characteristics of a traditional low-loft look. This type of batting produces good results and is a realistic compromise between cotton and polyester battings offering the advantages of both fibers.

Your choice of batting depends upon the finished look you want to give to your quilt. For a successful outcome, it is essential to always **read and follow the manufacturer's instructions** before you choose and use a quilt batting.

No matter what the fiber content, be aware that some people can be allergic to the chemicals used in surface treatment methods. If this is a concern, you can try one of the new batts with heat-treated surfaces.

What Size Batt Should You Purchase?

Purchase a batt that is at least 6" larger than your quilt—the same size you made your backing. The manufacturer prints the size of the batting on its packaging. Larger is better than smaller. You can always use leftover scraps in other small projects. Don't trim down your batting until after it's placed onto the backing during basting.

If you can't find a big enough batt or you have leftovers of the same fiber content you'd like to join and use, follow these simple instructions to make one large batt from smaller pieces.

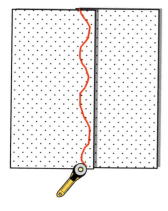

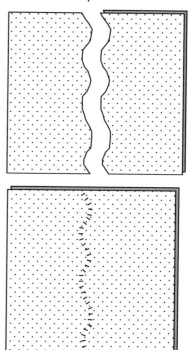

Step 1: Overlap batting pieces at least 2". Using your rotary cutter, cut a curvy line through BOTH batting pieces at the same time. Save scraps for stuffing pillows, etc.

Step 2: Butt the two curved edges together. They will match exactly because you cut them at the same time.

Step 3: With needle and matching thread, hand sew pieces together with large crisscross stitches (herringbone stitch). Don't pull the thread so tightly that it puckers the batting.

Okay, you're home with your 4-1/2 yards of backing material and quilt batt. You pre-shrank your quilt top fabrics; so don't forget to pre-shrink your backing fabric. A simple wet-down with warm water is sufficient. Be sure to check for color-fastness as you did before. If the fabric doesn't transfer color into the rinse water, wring it out and toss it in the dryer. If it does, rinse it until the water runs clear—or don't use it!

Now we're ready to transform the 4-1/2 yards of fabric into a backing. The first thing you will do is **tear it**! The tightly woven selvage edges need to be removed before we can sew the backing together. So, as we removed them in Lesson 7, tear off the selvage edges. Here we don't have to be concerned with distortion of the fabric pattern caused by tearing because all these torn edges will either be hidden by a 1/2" **seam** or trimmed off after the quilting process. Iron the yardage with no folds or creases.

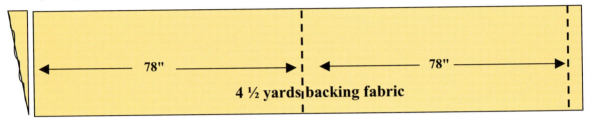

Square up one end of the backing fabric by tearing or cutting a straight edge across the width. Measure the **length** of your quilt plus 6" from the straightened end. For the example quilt, that measurement would be 78". Cut off 78". Measure and cut off a second length of 78". You now have two pieces of fabric that are each 6" longer than your quilt.

Add 6" to the **width** measurement of your quilt for shrinkage. The width of the example quilt is 57-1/2" plus 6" shrinkage allowance requires a backing width of 63-1/2". Each of the fabric pieces after removal of the selvage edges has about 43 useable inches, so we need to add at least 30" from the second piece to reach that goal. We mustn't forget to include seam allowances, and **these seams will be 1/2" wide**. Two seams will join four seam edges using 1/2", that's two more inches. We need to add 32" to the center fabric strip. Half of 32" is 16"— we will cut off two 16" lengths from the second piece of backing fabric. Keep the 11" strip of fabric in case you want to add a hanging sleeve to the back of your quilt later. (See Lesson 10, page 150)

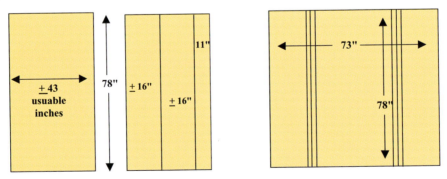

Using a 1/2" seam allowance, sew a 16" strip to each side of the 43" panel. Press the seams open. Those seams add extra bulk, and you don't want to quilt through five layers if pressed to one side.

We have our three layers—the top, the batting and the backing. We're ready for the next stop on the road to a completed quilt.

If you want to completely hand quilt your top, you will want to hand baste the layers together. Thread basting will not interfere with later securing the sandwich into a hoop or frame, a necessity for hand quilting. You will need guidance and help, so I encourage you to join a quilt club where you can find wonderful support and inspiration. Most quilt shops have a listing of clubs with contact names and telephone numbers within their sales areas.

Before machine quilting became a common way to attach a quilt top, batting, and backing, quilts were either tied or hand quilted using a basting frame and many quilting friends. These basting bees were a fun gathering for women, and one of the few social outlets available to them in the 1700s and 1800s. The old-fashioned basting frame consisted of four lengths of dimensional lumber, usually 2" x 2". These boards were covered with a sturdy, closely woven material such as canvas or denim, which stopped approximately 4" from each end and extended evenly along the length like a little "flap." Traditionally, two boards would be 8 ft. and the other two would be 10 ft. By sliding these boards back and forth perpendicular to each other, the frame could be adjusted to fit any size quilt. Four "C" clamps were used to hold these boards together at the corners, where great care was taken to ensure they were perfectly square.

After the frame was assembled, made square, and adjusted to fit the size quilt that was to be basted, it would be placed on the high backs of four chairs (seats facing toward the center of the frame) or attached to upright stanchions made for the purpose of supporting the frame.

Centers of each side of the frame were marked on the fabric coverings. Then centers were marked on each four sides of the quilt top and the backing fabric. Matching center points, the backing was stretched wrong side up and firmly pinned to the fabric flaps of the frame. Again, care was taken to ensure square corners.

Then the batting was unrolled and centered onto the backing fabric. Any necessary trimming of the batting was done at this time to make it the same size as the backing. With the quilt top facing right side up, its centers were aligned to those of the backing, and the top was carefully centered, smoothed, stretched over the batting, and pinned through to the backing. The whole stretched unit was tight enough to bounce a quarter tossed onto its surface.

Now the quilt could be basted! Many hands made light work, and a number of "needle basters" would take their positions at all four sides of the frame with their double-threaded long needles. They would take long, running stitches across the width and down the length of the quilt sandwich. These rows of stitches would be placed about a hand's-width apart. When the basters could no longer reach toward the center of the quilt, each short side, one at a time, would be released from the "C" clamps, and the basted part of the quilt would be carefully rolled onto the 8 ft. boards (one rolled over, one rolled under). Before re-attaching the "C" clamps, the accuracy of new "square" corners would again be checked. In this fashion, the quilt top would be completely basted with thread in a checkerboard pattern ready for hand quilting.

If the quilt were to be tied instead of basted, the volunteers would fill large-eyed needles with perle cotton, embroidery floss, or yarn, and the quilt would be "tied" to completion. The addition of a binding edge finish by its maker was all that remained to be done.

Today with so many women working, it is difficult to find the time to get together with fellow quilters to baste a quilt let alone to hand quilt it. That is why so many quilters have turned to pin basting and machine quilting.

Pin-Basting

One person can do pin basting, although the company of two or more helpers is definitely more enjoyable and easier on one's back and neck. Essentially, the same procedure as thread basting is followed with safety pins replacing needle and thread, and one or two long tables substituting for the basting frame.

You can use your dining room table fully extended with all its leaves. You'll have to cover your tabletop with a pad or cardboard to protect it from scratches. Many quilt shops have long tables and space available to quilters who want to pin baste their quilts. Also, churches and community centers that have long tables and recreation rooms are willing to let you use their facilities. Call for information. I find these organizations are very welcoming and accommodating.

I use the tables at my town's recreation center for basting. It's great fun, and passersby always stop to admire the quilts and learn about quiltmaking. I've even gotten interested visitors to become students, who are also now using the tables for their quilts.

We can't pin the backing edges to the table, so we use large binder clips for fastening the layers. These binder clips can be found at stationery and office supply stores and are inexpensive. They'll be stiff to open at first, but they will loosen up with use—for the **next** quilt. You'll need at least 12 clips.

Use #1 nickel-plated safety pins for the actual basting. The pin size is very important. It should be thin and very sharp so that no tiny broken thread holes will be made in your quilt top or backing. There are special basting pins available that have a bend in the closure part. The students in one of my classes did a comparison when pin-basting their quilts. We found that, with or without the bend, it made no difference on how difficult it was to close the pins. So if the specialty pins cost more, it's probably not worth the expense. I've found some very nice pins at the dollar-type store. Just make sure they're nickel-plated. You'll be using about 400 pins placed **3 to 4 inches apart** for the standard 60" x 75" quilt diagrammed in this book.

If you encounter a blunt safety pin while you're basting, throw it away. Also, as you remove a pin while machine quilting, don't close it again. Put the open pins in a secure container and store it away from children and pets. You'll find it an unnecessary bother to have to open pins as you are basting, and another bother to close them again after you remove them from your quilt only to open them again for the next basting. In fact, you can purchase "open" pins through catalogs, but they cost twice as much as "closed" ones!

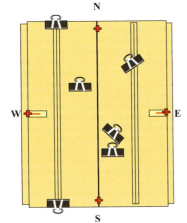

Setting Up for Pin Basting

First, find the centers on all four sides of your quilt backing and mark with a safety pin. Place a short strip of masking tape at the outside center edge of each side of the table(s). If you're using two tables, of course, the top and bottom centers will be where they meet. If the quilt is too small for two tables, center your backing onto one table with even amounts of overhang on opposite sides. I'll describe the basting procedure assuming the use of two long (6 ft.) tables pushed together.

Find the centers of the "west" and "east" table sides again. There should be a piece of masking tape there. Make a mark onto the masking tape at the exact center.

With the backing wrong side up, match backing center pins and table center marks. The E and W sides will probably hang over the table edges; so reset the backing center pins toward the middle until they meet the table markings. Make sure those adjusted backing side center points are accurate.

Using the binder clips, clamp the backing to the tables. If you have a helper, work in tandem across from each other. This will keep even tension on the backing as you secure it to the tables. If the binder clips can't catch the top and bottom edges of the quilt, secure them to the table with short strips of masking tape.

After securing all sides of the backing to the table, lay your prepared batting evenly on top of the backing, removing then reattaching each clamp to include the two layers. Be careful to keep the backing fabric smooth and undisturbed. If you know the batting is too large, arrange it so you'll only have to cut off excess from two sides. Doing this will result in larger scrap pieces that may be used later.

Finally, mark the edge centers of your **quilt top** with safety pins. Fold the top in half and carefully lay it over the batting. Open the top matching its centers to the centers of the backing. Smooth the top to remove wrinkles and square it up. Where you can, remove and reattach binder clips over the three layers without disturbing them. Clamp the quilt sandwich taut, but do not stretch it. If the top isn't as long as the tables and you can't secure its "north" and "south" edges, leave the backing and batting clipped or taped and secure only the "east" and "west" sides. We'll attach the top and bottom with pins.

You'll be bumping into the binder clip handles, so flip them over onto the quilt to get them out of the way.

Last Chance to Make Your Blocks Square

With your quilt sandwich clamped to the tables, this is the last chance you will have to affect how straight your blocks and sashing strips will look. We know that we made the quilt square with our careful measuring and attachment of lengthwise grain borders. Still, you might see less than straight lines either within or at the sashing edges of the blocks. We can fix this using our 15" square grid ruler.

To keep from having bloody fingers, insert the pin with your right hand, pushing toward your tummy, and close it with that thumb nail. If you insert the pin away from yourself, you'll have to close it with the forefinger and thumb of your other hand, which will get sore and bleed before all 400 pins are in position. If you're really having trouble with sore fingers, use the bowl of a spoon to help you close pins.

Use the 15" grid square ruler to test the **top center** of the quilt. Align the unclamped quilt top border edge and its seam to the table and secure though to the backing with pins. Adjust any sashing seams above the center block in the first row so they are parallel with the table edge and lines on the ruler and pin. Avoid pinning on top of seams, as you will be machine quilting them "in the ditch." If a seam is wavy, straighten it with your fingers and place a pin on **the side you moved the seam to**. If it's extra wavy, you may have to place many pins on both sides of a seam to keep it straight. Later, when you're quilting, the number of pins in an area will be a sign to you that a problem exists there, and you can hold the seam straight as you quilt.

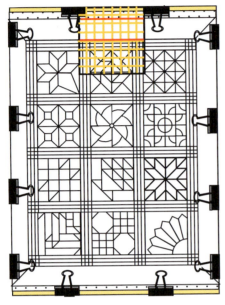

Align border edge and seam to table edge.

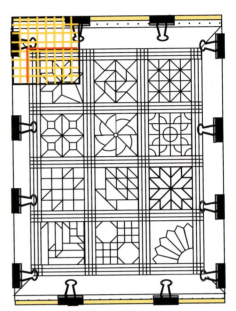

Square seams with table edges

Continue this same procedure as you move to adjust the left then right corners testing and squaring up the quilt edge and border seams with the table edges. Then invite your quilting buddy to work with you pinning the rest of the quilt. Sharing the grid ruler, work opposite each other here, too, in an organized fashion. **Always reference your grid ruler to seam lines you know are straight and square.**

The binder clips are not sacred, they can be moved. Occasionally, you may have to release and reclamp. The quilt may flatten as you're pinning causing the quilt/border seams to move towards the long sides of the table. That's okay; just keep seam lines straight and parallel with the sides of the table.

Basting within Blocks

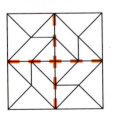

Move down to address the first row of blocks. Use the grid square to check the center block in that row, **Windblown Square**. At the same time, you'll be looking at the adjoining sashing to make sure it is also straight. The major axis lines within the block should be parallel to the sides. Make corrections, straighten seams, and pin baste the interior of the block. Also square up, check, and adjust the sashing strips, if necessary. Remember, pins are placed 3" to 4" apart and should be **filled** with quilt sandwich (take a good-sized bite) to keep the layers from shifting. If some patches within a block are a little too big after you adjust and pin its sides straight, gently pat down the puff of excess fabric and pin. Don't worry, it will quilt out.

The pin basting process continues by first pinning the center block of each successive row. Square its perimeter by referencing seams you know are accurate. Address patches within the block and make their seam lines **appear** straight. Move to the adjoining sashings to check for and adjust straight lines. Go to the blocks on each side; make any adjustments, then progress to its adjoining sashings. Finally, align the side border seam to the table edge.

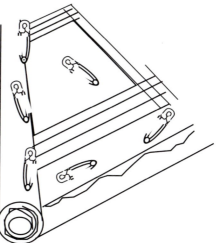

When you come to the bottom border, repeat the same procedure you used to square, straighten, and pin the top border. Make sure, also, that the pinned-side border seams are still parallel to the table edges.

Finally, stand at each side of your basted quilt and look down the rows of sashing strips for a final "straight" check. It doesn't have to be perfect; it just has to give the impression of being straight.

Remove the binder clips. I hope you have a few pins left because it's a good idea to roll and pin the extra backing over the batting and quilt edges. This protects them from fraying and catching on your sewing machine foot while quilting.

Next stop…Quilt Central!

You know, there are very nice people who will take your quilt top and pieced backing, supply the batting and machine quilt it for you. The cost depends upon the size and quilting design you choose. If you have this done with an overall quilting pattern that doesn't trace each blocks' design, pick a motif and thread color that doesn't detract from your piecing. Ask at your local quilt shop for a reference.

*L*ESSON 9
Quilting

Quilting

We have a little work ahead of us as we learn how to both hand and machine quilt. Treat this stage in completing your quilt as a job that will be both creatively and physically challenging.

You will need the following supplies to begin machine and hand quilting. Most of the items you have been using all along or have around your home. A few will be new to you. We'll begin with machine quilting.

• **Sewing machine** in good working order. Although a smaller featherweight-size sewing machine is wonderful for piecing, it is not heavy enough for machine quilting.

• **Walking or even-feed foot** for straight line, in-the-ditch machine quilting. This foot is indispensable; you cannot do a good job of machine quilting without it. Some brands are quite expensive. Mine was, and I had to view its purchase as a long-term investment in quality workmanship. Quilt shops and sewing catalogs carry generic models that may fit your machine. Follow the manufacturer's guidelines and instructions for attaching it.

- A good **14 (90) machine quilting needle**. These needles are especially made for quilting. If you cannot find the specific machine quilting needle, you can substitute a regular 14 (90) needle.

- Threads: **YLI Wonder Invisible Thread for top**; **dressmaker thread to match the backing in the bobbin.** Choose YLI "clear" if your fabrics are light; "smoke" if they are dark or intense. You may have to use both and change colors at times, depending upon the fabric colors in the areas you will be quilting. A **thread stocking** (small plastic net sleeve) will help control the YLI monofilament thread from unwinding.

- **Thread snips.** They're nice to have handy to snip the thread tails as you quilt.

- An old pair of **tweezers** will help you get out of tight situations with closed basting pins showing up in awkward positions.

- As you have been working with your fabrics, you may have noticed that your hands lose natural oils, become dry, and have less "traction." Also, "older" fingertips evidence the decline of pronounced fingerprint indentations caused by years of hard work and thinning skin. These factors make it more difficult to grip onto and guide your quilt's flat surfaces during machine quilting. That's why you need to use either **rubber fingers, latex gloves, cotton gloves with gripper dots made for machine quilting,** or **two 6" squares of mesh rubber shelf liner.**

The purpose of these little helpers is to aid you in holding the top surface of the quilt so you can slightly spread the seams apart as you stitch in-the-ditch. Each notion has its advantages and disadvantages. The gloves cover all your fingers. The latex gloves make your hands perspire; the cotton gloves don't. Mesh rubber shelf liner squares are helpful, but take some getting used to and can hide the target seams. I prefer the rubber fingers sold as quilting notions. You get eight progressive sizes in a package, and I use seven—none on the index finger of my right hand—so I can thread needles and feel for high or low sides of the seams. None are needed on either of your little fingers.

Keep a tiny "sample" container of talcum powder with your rubber gloves or fingers. When you finish a machine quilting session, dust the inside and outside with a little bit of the powder. This will absorb any moisture and keep the rubber surfaces from sticking together and ready for the next use.

- **Large rubber bands**, the kind the mail carrier bundles your mail with. Now you have a recycling use for them!

- Optional: **Bicycle clips** to hold the rolled-up edges of your quilt while you're quilting. You don't have to go to a bicycle shop; you can find these at quilt shops and fabric store notion displays. The metal clips won't work very well until they're wrapped with strips of leftover cotton fabric or muslin. All types lose their usefulness as the thickness of the rolled quilt edge they're holding diminishes.

- Place **a table or ironing board** alongside your sewing machine to help support the quilt as you work on it. You want to keep the weight of the quilt off the floor so it isn't pulling against the needle, making it difficult for you to sew.

- Optional: A **Quilter's table** is a clear, Plexiglass surface on short, adjustable legs that surrounds the bed of your sewing machine and expands the work area while supporting your quilt as you sew. It's another expensive quilting aid. You can machine quilt without it, but it's very helpful, especially if you later want to try free-motion machine quilting of decorative motifs in open areas. A quilter's table would be a very nice gift—hint to someone who might buy you one! Of course, if your sewing machine drops into a cabinet, you already have a larger area to work on.

Now is the time to begin planning for hand quilting designs; i.e., stencils. Initially, I have no idea what hand quilting motifs I'll put in the open areas of my quilts, but during the machine quilting process, the blocks begin to "tell" me what they need. At the end of this book you will find my offering of a few quilting designs for some of the blocks in this book.

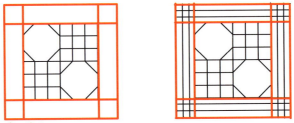

"In-the-Ditch" Machine Quilting

We will machine quilt the sashing seam lines that join to the blocks, indicated by the red lines in the illustrations. This will create a secure framework that will hold our three layers together as we add more machine or hand quilting within each block. (If your sashing is pieced, you need only quilt the seams that join the sashings to the blocks.) After the framework quilting is done, we will stitch along some of the seam lines within each block. All of this quilting will be done "in-the-ditch."

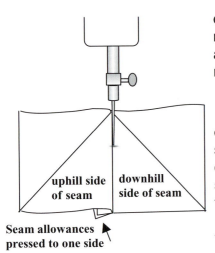

uphill side of seam   downhill side of seam

Seam allowances pressed to one side

The term "in-the-ditch" refers to quilting stitched almost right on top of the seam line. This type of quilting does not show and makes both the design and the background appear puffy. It can also be done by hand, but lends itself extremely well to machine quilting—especially by a beginner.

Because we pressed the seam allowances in our blocks in one direction, each seam line or "ditch" will have a high and low side. Your needle will automatically favor the downhill side of the ditch and, try as you may, you won't be able to make it sew a straight, invisible line on the uphill side. So don't fight it; go with the flow. **Always stitch in the downhill ditch.** That's one of the reasons I don't cover my right index finger; I want to be able to feel for the downhill side of seams. Sometimes those downhill sides aren't where you would expect them to be.

Physical Comfort and Well-Being

It won't take you long to understand the physical challenges of machine quilting, so let's start off with a few ergonomically correct rules. Dr. Susan Delaney Mech, author, quilter, and physician, recommends in her book, *Rx for Quilters: Stitcher Friendly Advice for Every Body*, that good posture is by far the most important factor in alleviating fatigue and muscle strain while you are quilting. Your chair should be adjusted so that your knees bend at a 90-degree angle and your feet rest flatly on the floor. You should provide lumbar support for the small of your back by either adjusting your chair or securing a small pillow to the back of your chair so that you can move your hips to the rear of the seat.

Your work surface should be about 4" below your bent elbow, which also should be at a 90-degree angle. Set your machine on a lower desk or table where your shoulders can be relaxed and your fingers rest lightly on the throat plate as your arms and hands guide the fabric. I have an armless secretary's chair, which I love. I can adjust the height up or down and move the back in close enough to force me to sit up straight. My husband bought me the chair at a used office furniture sale where he works. It's of higher quality than I would have bought for myself in a brand new chair.

Okay, we're sitting with feet flat on the floor and backs straight. Our shoulders and neck are relaxed. Well, don't sit there for too long! Dr. Mech also advises that we should stand up, walk around, drink a glass of water and perform a few stretching exercises once every hour for about 10 minutes. By doing this, she says you can expect to accomplish 25% more. I have to second that statement. With my neck injury, if I don't give myself regular breaks, I really suffer for it later, especially in loss of quilting time waiting for neck spasms to go away.

Another helpful hint from Dr. Mech before we begin: you may need more light to be able to see as you quilt either by hand or machine. Direct an extra lamp or task light over your work area to reduce eyestrain. Don't forget to wear your eyeglasses, too.

One last suggestion is that you should machine quilt early in the day when you're not tired. It's difficult to "drive" straight down those ditches—and more difficult when you're a little weary; don't forget those hourly breaks!

Quilters, Adjust Your Engines!

Let's adjust our sewing machine settings before we prepare our quilt sandwich. If you haven't already done so, attach the walking foot according to manufacturer's instructions. If your machine has a setting which allows you to choose whether it stops with the needle down or up, choose "down." Reduce the presser foot pressure slightly. Make adjustments to the stitch length, setting for approximately 8 to 10 stitches to an inch. Too long a stitch can be caught and broken; too short a stitch can cause tearing.

Check your settings to see what kind of stitches you'll get. Mimic your quilt sandwich by pinning together scraps of backing, batting, and a patch fabric of a size sufficient to practice on. Try quilting the practice piece with the walking foot to get a feel for the process. If necessary, make any further adjustments to the stitch length and presser foot so that the layers move securely and smoothly, and stitches are spaced approximately eight to an inch. Then write all your setting numbers on the sample with an indelible pen. Keep this record of your machine quilting settings as a reference for the next time. Don't forget to change the numbers if you later change adjustments.

If applicable, lower your ironing board and put it behind your sewing machine. If you have a low table, you can use that. You want to keep the weight of the rolled quilt up off the floor as it feeds out from under the needle so it won't engage you in a tug of war as you're trying to sew. If needed, use whatever additional support you can devise to carry the weight of the quilt.

Whenever you are machine quilting, always begin and end a line of stitching for 1/4" with the stitch length setting at almost "0" then return the length back to 8 stitches per inch. This will secure your thread ends so they cannot be pulled out.

Preparing the Sandwich for Quilting

First we will stitch the sashing seams in the ditch to isolate our quilt into four sections, just as if we had drawn imaginary lines from the center to the top, from the center to the bottom, and from the center to each side. Depending upon the layout of your quilt, you may or may not have seams exactly in the centers; therefore, treat the closest sashing seams that run from the exact middle to the borders as the center lines of your quilt.

To reduce the bulk to a manageable size and control overhang, we must "package" our quilt. We will use large rubber bands at the ends of each roll and bicycle clips wrapped with strips of cotton fabric to hold the middles. Wrapping keeps the clips from sliding and loosening their grip on the rolled quilt. Rubber banding the ends won't hurt the quilt.

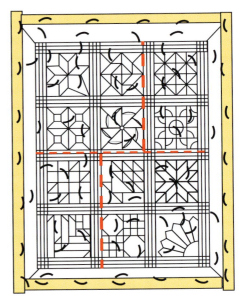

Diagram of quilt divided into quarter sections.

Evenly roll the right and left sides of your quilt and secure with rubber bands and bicycle clips leaving an area right down the middle exposed and flat as shown in the illustration below. The center to top and center to bottom quilting lines will be stitched first.

The First Line of Machine Quilting

To quilt the center-to-bottom seam, carefully slide the top flat area of your packaged quilt under the even feed foot and move to where the off-center starting point is under the needle. Support the top end on the ironing board, and hold the rest of the packaged quilt either in your lap or draped over your shoulder. Don't let the weight of the quilt drag.

Keep the exposed part of the quilt flat and don't let it shift. Drop the presser foot lever. Take one stitch to pull the bobbin thread through to the top and initially hold onto both the bobbin and top threads. Reduce the stitch length to almost "0" and stitch for 1/4" to secure the threads. If your machine has a "fix" feature, use that instead.

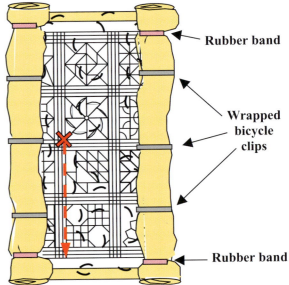

Rubber band

Wrapped bicycle clips

Rubber band

After you have completed the 1/4" locking stitches, place your hands on the quilt in front of and to the sides of the foot slightly fanning out your fingers (using rubber fingers/gloves/pads). Spread the uphill from the downhill sides exposing the seam line and helping the fabric remain pucker free as it is fed under the needle. Don't pull or push the fabric, let the walking foot and feed dogs do their job, just open a path on the seam line and guide the fabric as it moves along. Sew slowly; take your time. The needle has to go in and out of a thick layer of fabrics, and you want every stitch to be complete. You'll ultimately sew faster with more practice, and you'll definitely be getting more experience before you're finished!

Stitch close to the seam on the "downhill" side of the ditch from the center towards the bottom edge of your quilt. Again, your needle will automatically favor the "downhill" side of a seam. After quilting when the two sides of the seam come back together, your stitching will be hidden. If you have borders, stop just before them and lockstitch at almost "0" for 1/4", or use the fix feature. If you have no borders, you can stitch off the quilt edge with a backstitch.

When you anticipate stitching quite near a basting pin, remove it just in advance of getting too close. Don't think you'll be able to avoid it. Pins can get caught on the wider walking foot, when you won't be able to take them out easily and could chance tearing your quilt. Encountering trouble like this can affect the straightness of a seam, and one thing you don't want to do is start and stop a line of stitching if you don't have to. If this does happen, keep an old pair of tweezers nearby to help you open and remove the basting pin.

A concentration of basting pins in one area will be a sign that a major correction was made to a pin-basted seam. How will you make the correction? Hold the seam straight from behind as well as in front of the needle. Don't pull it, just hold it taut. If you really can't remove an upcoming pin because its positioning is crucial to keeping the seam straight, at least open it for removal at the last minute. You may have to sew this seam haltingly, starting and stopping to remove pins and make adjustments.

What If Your Stitching Goes Off-Track?

Depending upon which way seam allowances are pressed, you will have to "switch

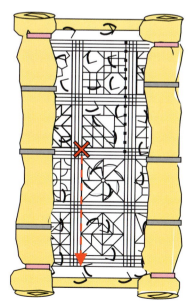

> Snip the top threads at the beginning and ending of a seam as you quilt. They're difficult to find later, and you don't want to stitch those tails down when you're quilting in a different direction. Be very careful not to cut the quilt top.

lanes" as you sew alongside patches and come to intersections. So go "jogging." When you come to an intersection where seam allowances change direction, simply slow down or stop, and move the quilt sandwich slightly to the left or right as you sew. The resulting "jog" will not be noticeable on the front, and barely noticeable, if at all, on the back.

If you see that your stitching is beginning to go where no other has gone before, STOP. Lift the foot and reposition the needle. You'll be surprised how unnoticeable the correcting point will be. If you're having a hard time "steering," you might be tired, or the seam allowance unexpectedly flipped and you're trying to stitch on the uphill side of the ditch. Don't fret over a few misplaced stitches. You may know where they are, but no one else will even see them.

After this first seam is completed, remove your quilt and rotate it, being careful not to create wrinkles in the backing. Machine quilt the center to top seam.

Now you can unroll the left and right sides of your quilt, and roll and secure the top and bottom sides toward the center, leaving a flat area sideways across the middle in which to quilt the crosswise center lines.

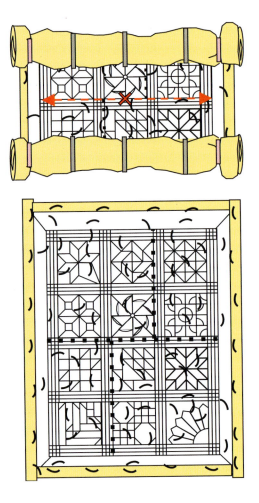

Quilt the crosswise centers from the middle out to each side.

You have now isolated your quilt into four sections. Open it up and check the back for any glaring errors and sewn-in wrinkles. If you see a wrinkle, evaluate how noticeable it is against the busy print of the backing. If it's minor, ignore it. If you see a large tuck of backing fabric, remove only as much of the stitching as you need to release it. Smooth out the fabric and iron out the wrinkle. This is important because the wrinkled fabric has a memory, and you could get another tuck on that seam when you re-quilt it.

Pin-baste the affected area on the **backing**. You know where you'll have to quilt the replacement seam, so don't place pins in the path of the bottom feed dogs. Turn the quilt right side up and, using the beginning and ending lockstitch over the thread that remained, re-quilt the removed seam. Clip thread tails and remove back pins.

Using the same techniques you have just learned, you can now prepare to machine quilt each "quarter" of your quilt. Always start at the original middle crosswise or lengthwise quilted lines of the entire quilt, not in the middle of one of the quarters.

To machine quilt sashing seams in each quarter, roll and band one side of your quilt. You can loosely roll any other sides if that will help you, or you can leave them free.

Let's use the quilt's lower right quadrant as an example.

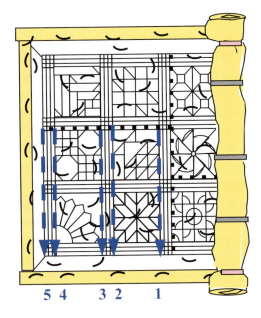

5 4   3 2   1

With the quilt packaged in the configuration shown on the previous page, machine quilt lines **1, 2, 3, 4, and 5**, **in that order.** The rolled edge will be hard to maneuver because it will rest under the machine arm, so wrap it tightly.

You will have to repackage to sew lines **6, 7, 8, and 9**, **in that order too**, but with no bulky quilt roll under the machine arm.

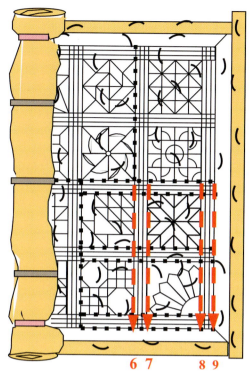

You can see that to keep the quilt square and eliminate bunching and catching puckers in the backing, all quilting lines must be sewn away from the lengthwise and crosswise center lines of the quilt. Sometimes you will have a large, bulky roll of quilt under your machine's arm; other times you won't. Do the best you can. Once you have all the sashing/block seams quilted, you will be able to machine quilt within the blocks in relative freedom from rolling. So finish quilting the sashing seams in the other three sections, then we'll move on to quilting the blocks.

Machine Quilting in the Blocks

The blocks also will be machine quilted in the ditch following some of its design elements. You don't have to machine quilt all the seam lines. The only restriction you really have is the one spelled out by the quilting distance requirements of the batting. Since we will be machine and hand quilting, we'll let both methods satisfy the restriction.

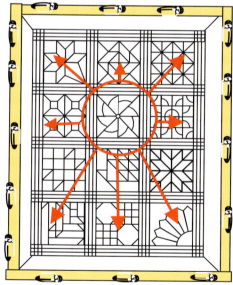

The in-the-ditch sash quilting has provided a framework to keep the quilt layers from shifting, but puckers can still occur when sewing within the blocks. I usually begin by stitching within a middle block of my quilt, progressively working out to adjoining blocks. Quilting blocks from the middle out limits shifting and stitched-in wrinkles.

When you are quilting the middle block(s), you'll have to roll and secure the side that will lie under the machine arm. Nothing formal, just keep the bulk confined. Give yourself an unencumbered flat plane to work on by arranging, smoothing, and flattening the block you will be stitching. Feel for any wrinkles or puckers on the backing before sewing.

Quilt the major intersecting lines of each block first. This is just another orderly step to prevent shifting and wrinkles. You do not have to sew these lines from the center out as you did when quilting the sashing seams; edge-to-edge is fine. Remove basting pins as usual.

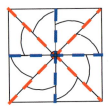

Spinning Pinwheel is one of the center blocks in the example quilt. It has two sets of intersecting seams. I would quilt both the diagonals and the N-S, E-W seams, but I would leave the curves and the rest of the block available for the addition of a little hand quilting. There, one block is done!

Sometimes a block's major intersecting lines are difficult to determine or there really aren't any at all. In **Grandmother's Fan**, for example, I would make sure the block was pinned securely because it contains a large, flexible open space that I'd want to hand quilt later. Well-placed basting pins will have to hold it for machine quilting. Stitch all the seams in-the-ditch: the zigzag line of the fan tips, the curve of the fan base and the seams joining each fan blade.

You're finally able to pivot the quilt while stitching to reduce the number of starts and stops. Keep the needle in the "down" stopping position, or turn the flywheel to insert the needle into the layers before you release the presser foot to turn your work. It's fun to figure out how far you can go with one beginning and one ending lockstitch.

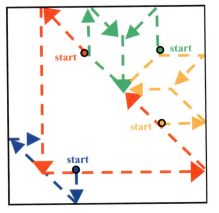

You don't have to cut the invisible thread after you lockstitch each continuous quilting line. Just move to the next starting point, 1/4" lockstitch, and sew on to the next ending lockstitch. You'll want to cut the thread tails occasionally while you are quilting so the even feed foot doesn't get caught up on them. While checking for puckers, cut all the tails, back and front, after you complete machine quilting each block.

> If the nylon top thread breaks at an inopportune time and you have difficulty re-threading, hold a small piece of white paper behind the needle to make it easier to see the needle's eye.

Why Stop Now When We're Having So Much Fun?

You could call an end to your quilting at this point as long as your quilt's open, and unquilted areas are within the parameters recommended by the manufacturer of the batting you used. But by adding hand quilting after the machine work is done, your quilt will give the impression of being completely hand quilted.

Hand Quilting Supplies

The tools used for hand quilting haven't changed in over three centuries. There have been a few innovative aids developed to make hand quilting a little easier, but the basic thread, needle, thimble, and hoop are all you really need. See the photograph at the beginning of this lesson for a display of these supplies:

• **Hoops:** There are many types, sizes, and shapes of quilting hoops. Every quilter has a favorite. There are round, oval, and rounded square hoops made of wood or plastic, large and small. There are "fanny" hoops that are supported by a short pedestal that lifts the weight of your quilt up off your lap. There is even a special border hoop. (When you are ready to quilt your border, don't deny yourself this special tool.) Additionally, you can purchase wooden floor stands to which you can attach your quilting hoops for "lap-free" quilting.

I have found that too large a hand-held hoop is difficult to balance and reach across. My favorite hand-quilting hoop is oval and about 20" at its longest dimension and 13" at its shortest. This size and shape is excellent especially if you have some physical limitations that might prevent you from extending your head over a floor frame. Sitting in a comfortable position, you can place your feet on a footstool, balance the hoop on your knees, lean your head back and still quilt.

Before you choose the hoop that's right for you, test out different sizes and types. Ask your quilting friends if you could use one of theirs to see how it fits your style. Your hoop will become one of your favorite tools—a personal and comfortable "friend."

> No matter what hoop you use, you must always remember to remove your quilt from it at the end of each quilting session. If you leave your quilt stretched in a hoop for any length of time, portions of it can become distorted and stretched out of shape.

You don't have to use a hoop to quilt, although it certainly makes the task easier once you've learned how to use it. The "no hoop" method of hand quilting, sometimes referred to as lap quilting, may feel more comfortable when you are first learning to quilt because you can also use your non-dominant hand to manipulate the quilt "sandwich" onto the needle with each stitch.

In 1988, during the Reagan administration, President and Mrs. Reagan chose a quilt made by Julia H. Spidell of Sparta, NC, as a gift from the United States to Soviet Premier Mikhail Gorbachev and his wife Raisa. Julia's 90" x 90" gorgeous "Piece Baskets" quilt was entirely lap quilted with no hoop! Julia came to quilting with a background in art education. To find a way to make additional income while caring for her handicapped husband at home, she began quilting. Little did she know just how good a quilter she was! Julia is one of my personal heroes and an example of what quilting is all about: creating a quilt or a life out of the "materials" given to you. 2

- **Thimbles:** There is an ever-growing selection of thimbles. The benchmark thimble for hand quilting is made of metal with an indented top encircled by a raised ridge. This "lip" catches the quilting needle and helps you reinsert it back into the quilt. Usually, a thimble is worn on the middle finger of your dominant hand. The direction of quilting is across your body from either right to left (if you're a "righty"), left to right (if you're a "lefty") and towards yourself. Some very experienced quilters can quilt away from themselves using only a thimble on their dominant thumb. (I can't even do this, but I sure wish I could. More practice called for here.)

You will use the fingers of your "underhand" to feel for the needle tip as you stitch to be sure the needle has penetrated all three quilt layers. These repetitive little needle sticks can eventually sting, but you'll soon develop calluses on your fingertips—a recognition and badge of honor among quilters. To protect your "underhand" fingers, you can use wraps, oval self-stick protective plastic shields, or leather, metal and small plastic thimbles to deflect the needle back up through your quilt as you are quilting. Additionally, the use of a rubber fingertip on your index finger helps you grab and pull a stubborn quilting needle through your quilt.

My favorite is an inexpensive flesh-colored plastic thimble made especially for those quilters who have longer fingernails. This thimble can also be warmed and stretched to fit over arthritic knuckles. It has an open, adjustable side that allows for circulation of air.

I mentioned in the machine quilting section how constantly handling fabrics removes natural oils from your fingers and hands. For dry sore hands, two wonderful products to include in your sewing basket are Bag Balm® or Udder Cream®. Yes, these are repackaged bovine products, but they're great for us quilters. Bag balm is a salve that contains antiseptic and is so healing for sore fingers. Udder cream is also soothing for dry hands and is not greasy or sticky.

An occupational hazard of hand quilting is pricked fingers. It's a trade secret, but if you get a drop of blood on your quilt, your own saliva is the best solvent. Just dab a little cold water on the spot after removal to avoid later discoloration.

- **Needles and Threads** : Historically, the quilt stitch is executed with a single strand of thread and a sharp, thin, very short needle called a "between." The shorter the needle, the smaller and closer together you can work the stitches. It's always a balancing act between hand quilting skill and how small a needle eye we can thread when choosing the size of quilting needle to use. Betweens come in sizes from #3 through #12—the largest number is the smallest needle. Most experienced quilters use betweens in the #8 to #12 range.

Quilting needles are made of tempered steel, gold, or platinum. Choose good quality, realistically priced needles because they all break. As you quilt, you will notice that your needle may develop a "bend," which I like because it bends to fit my fingers. Of course, with use that "bend" eventually breaks, and you start over again with a new needle. Needles, too, become dull. If stitching becomes more difficult, it's probably time to replace the needle.

Quilting thread is made from strong, long cotton fibers that have been treated to make its surface glide through the layers of your quilt. It is the thread of choice. But you are not restricted to using *only* quilting thread. You can use embroidery and decorative threads as additional design elements to accent different areas of your quilt. Care should be taken when using these specialty threads because they are more fragile than quilting thread. You may not be able to load your needle with a very long strand because of breaking and fraying.

For the quilt we will be making in these lessons, I would like you to use single strands of **size #8 Perle Cotton,** an unorthodox thread for quilting. The look that thicker perle cotton gives longer beginner stitches is very pleasing, decorative, and more substantial than quilting thread. You will find the perle cotton in needlework and yarn shops. Also, some fabric and quilt shops might carry it in limited colors. It is inexpensive, and one ball is more than enough for a whole quilt—the way we do it.

Because of the thickness of perle cotton, you'll have to use a needle with a large eye, so try betweens in sizes #5, #6, or maybe #7. It's difficult to find the larger betweens in packets of all the same size, but packages of mixed sizes will contain the larger ones.

I find that beginners have a hard time executing the 10—12 stitches per inch of traditional hand quilting. They worry about evenness and how close the stitches are to each other. You cannot get close stitches using a #5 or #6 between and size #8 perle cotton thread! Experience with students, and my own work, has led me to encourage the revival of the old-fashioned "Depression" stitch in favor of getting hand quilting done more quickly. From its' name, you probably realized that the Depression stitch was born in that period of our country's history. This simple, larger quilting stitch made it possible then, and now, to finish quilts in less time.

- Don't forget **needle threaders**. There's a reason why four needle threaders come in some packages. They are going to break because we will put them through the difficult task of squeezing a fat thread through the needle's eye. (Hold onto the wire part as you pull the thread through the eye.) Buy a few packages of needle threaders. Don't buy the fancy ones for this project. Save the "fancies" for use later with regulation quilting and sewing threads.

- **Thread Heaven® or beeswax** add additional conditioning to the perle cotton or any quilting threads. Stroking your thread over either one lubricates it and allows it to glide more easily through the fabric, reducing tangling, fraying, and breaking.

- **Fabric marking implements:** Water or air-erasable pens, chalk, or white charcoal art pencils, wash-out pencils of appropriate colors, **pencil sharpener** (sharp points are very important for accuracy), soap sliver, .5 mm mechanical lead pencil, etc. As usual, test your marking instrument on a fabric sample to make sure it will wash out.

- **File folders and freezer paper** to help you transfer designs to the quilt top.

- **Stencils and quilting designs**: Choose quilting designs that compliment each patchwork block and the borders. There is a large sheet of stencils in the back of this book designed specifically for the blocks we have created. There are innumerable resources available to you for stencil patterns in stores, books, and magazines, even on the Internet at some quilt-related Web sites. You can also use some of your templates for quilting designs. You can buy plastic quilting stencils, or you can make your own. (More about that later.) Helen Squire, a well-known quilter and author, has written a series of large, inexpensive, very user-friendly stencil pattern books containing beautiful and easy-to-execute designs. I highly recommend her patterns and instructions to new quilters.

How Much Quilting? Fill the Spaces ....

As we've noted, the manufacturer of your batting has determined how close you need to place your lines of quilting. Since you have already machine stitched most of the seams in your top, you really won't have too many open spaces in which to hand quilt. Looking at the example Gold and Black Sampler, you can see that some blocks have more open areas than others. **Pinwheel** has no large open areas that require hand quilting. **Grandmother's Fan**, on the other hand, has a large area that would be enhanced with a quilting motif.

There are a few fundamental and practical rules for hand quilting:

1. If it won't show, don't put much time and effort into hand quilting an area. A large, darkly colored or highly patterned patch like the handle in **Bouquet of Flowers,** needs some quilting to meet the batting requirements, but that quilting just won't show very much unless its done with contrasting thread. A basic one or two-inch grid will hold the layers together, and add texture without consuming too much quilting effort.

The colorful diamond "flowers" will also hide any decorative quilting designs, but their area is still too large to leave unquilted. Simple outline stitching placed a little more than 1/4" away from the seam line will do the job here. Why +1/4"? Because you won't want to quilt through seam allowances where you don't have to. The background patches are also quilted with an outline that follows the seams. Their areas needed more quilting for balance, so a double outline was used.

2. If you want your quilting to show, use a contrasting color thread. Conversely, if you don't want your quilting to appear pronounced until you get better at it, use a color thread that will blend in with the background fabric.

3. A quilting design that fills open areas looks better than one that is too small, *and*, more importantly, larger designs are easier to quilt.

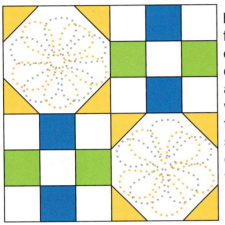

The two open hexagons in **Snowball and Nine-Patch** begged for a decorative quilting motif. I designed the flower for this block and quilted it in white perle cotton just as a first quilter with not too much confidence in her ability might do. I didn't want the quilting to stand out, but I also didn't want the area to look empty! Well, it looked empty and out of balance with the other elements of the block. Far be it from me to take out perfectly good quilting stitches! I just rotated the stencil and traced another flower on top of the first, then quilted it using tan perle cotton. The resulting double flower was even better than the single one. A happy accident!

Blocks have to be quilted enough to hold the batting and also contain an equivalent *sum* of machine and hand quilting to look balanced with other blocks and itself.

Marking the Blocks for Quilting

There are many marking tools to transfer quilting patterns to your quilt. If the fabric you are working on is dark, I recommend a white charcoal or white chalk pencil that can be sharpened to a fine point. For lighter fabrics, you may choose to use a wash-out marker, an air-erasable pen, or one of the many other marking instruments available today. You could even try a "pouncer" (a cloth bag filled with powdered chalk) when using a quilter's stencil. No matter which way you mark your top, no one method is perfect for every application. Chalk shows very well on darker patches but has a very short marking "life," and will brush off easily as you work. Lines made by water- or air-erasable pens will become permanent if exposed to heat or reappear after time if not completely washed out.

I prefer to use my old faithful .5mm mechanical lead pencil with HB or H lead for a marking tool. The lines created with a light touch of this pencil hardly show after quilting, and can be easily washed out. In any event, try your marking instruments on a sample of your fabrics to ensure they can be removed.

You can mark your basted quilt as you go along (that's what I usually do), or you can completely mark your quilt top before basting. Hold the stencil tight against the quilt top to reduce distortion as you trace. A few pieces of masking tape will help hold it in place. Use a delicate touch when marking.

Stencils

You can purchase plastic stencils or you can make your own. A grid stencil is a lot of trouble to make with all it's "bridges" to hold its cutouts together, so it's a good idea to purchase one. Stencils of other shapes are easy to make or trace from many sources. I transfer my designs onto manila file folders and outline them with indelible black pen. Instead of cutting slots, sometimes I cut the designs out individually.

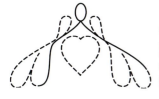

The illustration at the right represents the stencil for the open area in **Grandmother's Fan**. I drew it onto the paper side of a piece of freezer paper. I cut out the freezer paper pattern then ironed it, shiny side down, onto the block. I outlined the design with my .5mm pencil, then removed the stencil to use again. The freezer paper will not leave any residue.

Hooping it Up

As we did with machine quilting, we will begin hand quilting in the center of our quilt. Loosen the screw that holds the ends of the outer hoop together and separate the two pieces. With the right side of your quilt facing up, place the inner hoop under the exact center. Overlay the outer hoop with the screw clamp away from your body (so thread won't get tangled in it as you quilt) and press it down around the inside hoop. Pull at the edges of the quilt extending past the outer hoop to square up the block, and tighten the quilt over the inner hoop. When the center area is straight, smooth, and taut, tighten the hoop screw. You want the area of the quilt contained in the hoop to be under tension but still have a little "give." If you're going to mark your blocks as you quilt, it's easier to do so with the quilt in the hoop.

Itching to Stitch

Insert the end of a strand of perle cotton 6" beyond the needle's eye with the help of the needle threader. Unspool a length of thread that reaches from your fingers to your elbow and cut off. You'll be able to work this length (approximately 18") of thread into your quilt before it begins to fray and break. Not only does repeatedly being sewn through the quilt sandwich wear on the thread, so does traveling through the needle's eye. It's a good idea to occasionally slide the needle to different positions along the thread to reduce wear and tear. Your thread will twist after you've quilted for a while, so stop, invert the hoop, let the thread and needle dangle to unwind.

> Always use thread as it unwinds, tying a knot in the end that came off the spool last. Thread is wound onto the spool with a warp. If you were to sew against that warp, your thread would continually tangle, twist and knot.

With your thimble on and your needle threaded you are now ready to quilt! I hope you are sitting in a comfortable chair that gives good back support. A small footstool that raises your knees helps to reduce fatigue and improve your posture. Good light is a must. Remember what Dr. Mech says, only quilt for an hour, then get up and walk around to give yourself a break. You'll be much more productive when you return.

Don't expect to become an instant expert quilter. Quilt stitching skill comes only with time and practice. Require no more from yourself than to just relax and enjoy the rhythm of placing running stitches in and out of your quilt top. Don't try to make your stitches too close together, but do try to make them evenly spaced. Four or five to an inch is perfect. And don't think the stitches on the back have to be the same size as those on the front.

For all the rules and techniques you have been learning in quiltmaking, there are very few for actual hand quilting. The needle goes in; the needle touches your "underhand" finger; the needle comes out; the needle goes in again. Hand quilting is a skill you basically teach yourself, and learning to quilt is like learning to roller skate: your progress is slow in the beginning, but soon you'll be zipping along with speed and rhythm. You'll find hand quilting is very relaxing—and portable!

Eventually, you will switch to a smaller needle and regular quilting thread to achieve tinier, more uniform stitches. To get to that point faster, purchase a magnifying lamp and look through the lens as you quilt. You'll be surprised how quickly your stitches improve because it's much easier to see.

Knots!

Continuous lines of hand quilting are secured at the beginning and end by imbedding just the right size knot in the batting layer of the quilt. Let's learn how to make this quilter's knot.

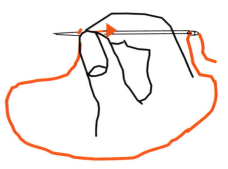

Hold your threaded needle between your forefinger and thumb. Take the "tail" end of the thread with your left hand and make it into a circle, laying the tail on top of the needle and pointing toward the eye. Pinch the thread end against the needle with the right fingers. With your left hand, wrap the thread around the needle tip four or five times for regular quilting thread, two times for perle cotton. Move your right hand fingers up to pinch the coil of thread that is wrapped around the needle. Now, take your left hand, and pull the needle through the pinched coil, and slide the coil down the thread length to the end. A nice, tight "quilter's knot" will be formed. If the leftover tail is too long past the knot, snip it off.

Because the perle cotton thread is thicker than normal quilting thread, it presents a problem when it comes to hiding knots. There are two ways to resolve this problem, and you'll use both during the course of your hand quilting. The knotted ends are going to need a little assistance going though the top of your quilt, so help it by enlarging the weave with the tip of your needle—just stick the needle in between threads and wiggle it. This insertion point should be about 3/4" away from where you want to start stitching to give the knot a little distance in which to catch and entwine itself within the batting. Slide the needle tip to where you want to begin quilting and bring it out. "Scratch" the tiny opening closed.

With a rocking motion, take even running stitches, gathering about four onto your needle before you pull the thread through. With each stitch, the needle should go through the backing where it will touch one of your fingers. Your "underhand" finger will feel that the needle has gone completely through the layers to make a good stitch. In one with this motion, help the needle back through the quilt layers to the top with an "underhand" finger (or thumbnail).

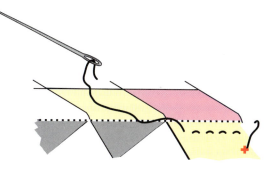

Ending a Line of Stitching with a Knot

When you see you are running out of thread, make that same quilter's knot close to the last "out" stitch. Wiggle an opening in the weave at the correct distance to finish the stitch. Insert the needle into the batting and bring the needle back out about 3/4" away. Tug the knot below the first layer. You might hear a little "pop" as the knot is pulled into the batting. Pull gently on the threaded needle, and hold your snips or scissors slightly open right on the thread but don't cut it by moving the snips or scissors; cut the thread by moving it into the blades. When your scissors are so close to the surface, it's too easy to accidentally cut the top. The tension of the taut thread end on the blade of your snips or scissors will cut the thread, and the thread will relax and slip under the surface of your quilt. Scratch the entry hole closed.

No Knots!

You can quilt with "no knots" by beginning and ending a line of stitching with a series of minute backstitches hidden in a seam line. Insert your needle into the top layer of your quilt an inch or so away from where you wish to start stitching. Bring the needle out right in the middle of a nearby seam line and pull the thread only until the tail end disappears under the quilt surface. Take a very small backstitch again in the seam line hiding the stitch as you tighten it. Don't pull too hard; this stitch doesn't have to be too tight, it's just the anchor. Repeat this procedure two more times. As you place each new backstitch, you can pull a little harder and see that the stitches won't pull out. When you exit your final backstitch you should be at the point where you wanted to begin your line of quilting.

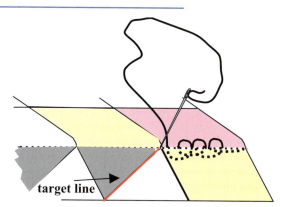

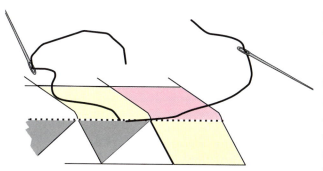

Expanding on the no-knot method, cut a piece of thread twice as long as the finger-to-elbow length, and load two needles on it. Take one stitch in the middle of the line of stitching you want to do, and pull the thread halfway through so that you have half the thread length and one needle on each side of the entry point. Then you can stitch with both ends. (I know I said you should thread your needle from the spool as it was wound, but this is one trick that breaks the rule. I'd rather deal with a few tangles to reduce the number of knots. Use the thread conditioner to limit twisting.)

Ending a No-Knot Line of Quilting

My preferred ending of a line of stitching is using the same backstitch method. You have to anticipate when you're going to run out of thread, and allow yourself enough length to secure the last inch or so within a nearby seam. Take a backstitch as your last running stitch, then slide your needle through the batting between the top and backing to a nearby seam. Take a series of three invisible in-the-ditch backstitches in the same manner as you began your quilting line. Tug on the threaded needle and snip the thread so the clipped end will slide below the quilt surface.

Traveling

If you have quite a bit of thread on your needle at the end of a line of quilting, traveling is how to get your thread from where it is to where you want to be. All you have to do after you secure the last quilting stitch with a backstitch is slide the needle between the layers to its destination. If the distance is further than the needle is long, slide the needle as far as you can in the right direction. Do the weave-opening trick to bring the needle up through the top, then return the needle back in the same hole and close it with your fingernail until you get to the next starting point. If the distance is ridiculously long, it's better to end the stitching and start over. I always check the quilt back after a traveling stitch to be sure it didn't come through to the backing.

Stabbing

Quilting though layered seam allowances is unavoidable, and you'll have to use a different quilting stitch called "stabbing." This entails making single stitches when crossing seams by perpendicularly inserting the needle all the way through to the back and returning it to the top of the quilt with your underhand. You may want to switch hands and use your "smart" hand underneath. This is where using the rubber finger really comes in handy. Pulling the needle and perle cotton thread through all those layers will take determination. Some quilters use this stitch exclusively. Ouch!

A Few More Random Thoughts

• You can end lines of quilting on the back as well as the front using either the knot or no-knot methods. For the no-knot method, just hide the tiny backstitches on a part of the backing fabric design that matches your thread.
• Don't worry about not getting one little stitch all the way through to the back—it's just one little stitch, and the front of the quilt is what you're interested in.
• Use a number of needles going in different directions within one hooped area as you quilt. This reduces starts and stops, and you can continue those same loaded needles into the next hooped area.
• As you hand quilt, you'll find and can cut off the machine quilting thread ends you missed.
• Always rotate the hoop to a comfortable quilting angle.
• If you quilt one block a night or one border in two nights, you should be able to finish a 12-block quilt in approximately two weeks of evenings. Think about your next quilt project while you're finishing this one.
• Finally, you don't want hand quilting to be perfect, you want it to look hand done.

Quilting the Border

When you've finished hand quilting the blocks that need it, you'll want to quilt the border. This quilting in particular convinces others that your quilt has been completely hand quilted. Prior planning is required to mark borders with a quilting design. Choose a simple, widely spaced motif that is at least 3/4" smaller than the border width so you won't have to quilt through seam allowances. I've included two easy ones in the back of the book. To use one, trace it onto an open manila file folder and cut out on the dashed lines. If the design crosses over the fold, tape it on both sides for reinforcement.

The quilting motif must be centered on each side. All ends must match to be worked into a corner design. I like to use freezer paper to plan and draw my border layout because I can get 72 and more uninterrupted inches to draw on. (That's not the only reason I use freezer paper. More on that coming up.)

To make your border layout, cut off a length of freezer paper that measures the length of your top before the borders were added and cut it down to a strip that is 2" wider than the border width. Draw a line 2" away from one long side. Fold the paper strip in half across the width. Open it and center your border stencil on the fold line. Place pencil marks on the paper at the ends of the design, then "space out" the stencil aligning end marks along the full length of the strip. Does the design or any of its repetitive parts fit evenly on the border layout? If it does, great! If not, you'll have to make adjustments to the design, which probably will be nothing more than adding or subtracting space between design element repeats, not whole stencil repeats.

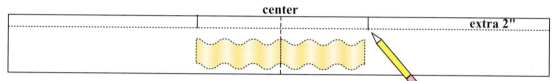

Align this edge to border/block seam

As you trace your layout plan, use the extra 2" we added to make notations on how you adjusted the stencil. Remember, your quilt should look hand made, not manufactured.

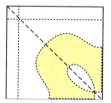

You'll need to plan on how you will turn the corner with your quilting design. Cut a square of freezer paper the measurement of your border width plus 2". (A 4" border will need a 6" square.) Transfer your corner design onto the freezer paper square, aligning diagonal centers. The outside edges that will join to the border must align.

Match your border layout to your corner and make any adjustments you feel are necessary. That's it! You've made your plan. By folding, you can adapt this layout plan to fit the shorter border and won't have to make two. Just use the 2" area to write instructions to yourself for changes. Using the file folder stencil, trace your design with an appropriate removable marking instrument onto the border fabric following your adjustment instructions.

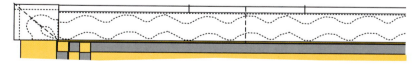

Do you recall that I showed you how to cut a small quilting motif out of freezer paper so you could iron it onto **Grandmother's Fan** and trace around it? Well, you can use this same idea and machine quilt your borders. You'll have to make four correctly sized border and corner patterns, because you will iron them in place and machine quilt right through them! Do one border and corner at a time. I like to use double decorative threads, like Sulky Ultra Twist®️ through the needle. It makes a better-looking stitch. Carefully tear the paper away after you finish each side.

For the Free Spirit

Here's an old, tried-and-true pattern to use called "teacups" that requires no planning ahead, but you have to like the random look. The stencil is made by drawing around a teacup onto a piece of lightweight cardboard. Cut out and fold the circle into quarters, notching the outside ends of each fold line. Now you can use this stencil to experiment and create an easy design for your border. Line the circles and notches up to each other in any way. Doing so will create rhythm to your design. You can draw and quilt one circle at a time.

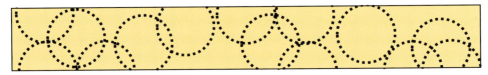

You don't have to do anything to the borders if the space between the blocks and the outside edge is less than the quilting distance required by the batting, but quilting looks so lovely.

Hand Quilting the Border

The quilt hoop to the right is especially made for quilting borders. It's a perfect example of the right tool for the right job. The raw edge of the border is safety pinned to the strip of heavy white fabric that is stapled to the wooden frame.

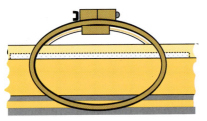

You can see that our favorite oval frame falls short in its ability to keep the border taut for hand quilting. But we can fix that.

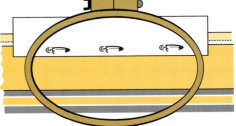

Pin a rectangle of tightly woven, doubled-over fabric to the border edge you will be quilting. Then place that area in your hoop. The added fabric strip has to be about as thick as the quilt layers for the hoop to hold it tightly.

Hand quilt the border design. You'll find it's enjoyably easy to do because you only have to cross seams at the corners. Also, start and end each line of stitching at the raw edge so you don't have to deal with hiding knots … we'll let the binding do that!

Can you believe it? After you complete quilting your borders, all there is left to do is add a hanging strip (if you would like), bind the edges, and add a label … the next lesson.

Chong Blind has been my friend for over 30 years A career woman, she always wondered why I would cut up fabric into little pieces, then sew them back together to make a blanket. She finally took my class and made this striking sampler, which she completely finished the day after her last class!

LESSON 10

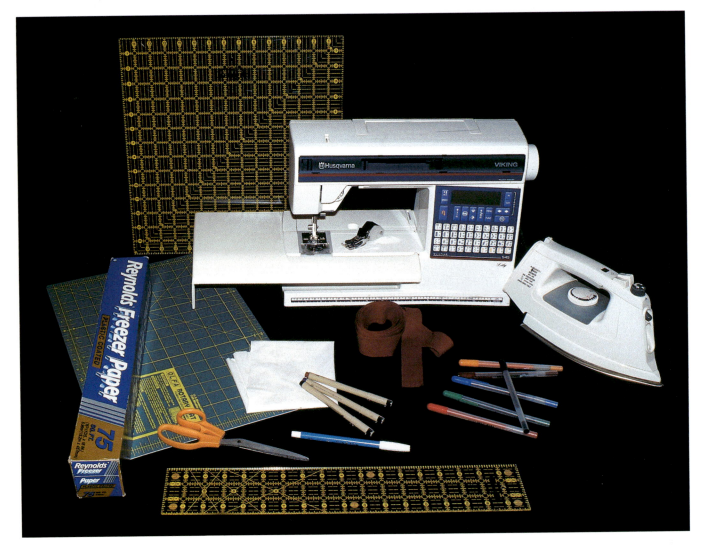

We will be using these supplies to finish our quilt:

- Sewing machine
- Binding fabric
- Rotary rulers and cutter
- Fabric and paper scissors
- Pins
- Removable marking instruments

- Freezer paper
- Scrap of tightly woven cotton for label
- Fabric markers or gel pens
- OPTIONAL: Backing fabric for sleeve

Cutting Off the Excess Batting and Backing

Let's take a look at our almost completed quilt. Are the **quilt top** corners still square? Do the sides wiggle? Use your large grid rulers to check.

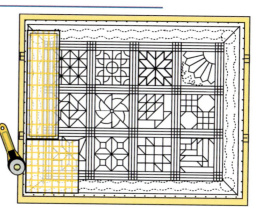

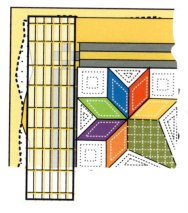

You may have to make a few corrections that could include "borrowing" batting and backing to make the sides straight. The binding we will apply to finish the quilt edges should be filled with batting and fabric, otherwise it will wear too easily. Don't be concerned if you have to cut away a little of the border fabric to straighten the sides and make the corners "square." The quilting process caused these changes.

You can use your rotary cutter, ruler and mat or good old-fashioned scissors for trimming. If you use the rotary cutter, place the rulers on top of the quilt to protect it as you cut away the backing and batting. If you want to be extra cautious, draw the cutting lines and use scissors. *Optional*: you can machine baste a scant 1/4" line of stitching all around the outside edges after trimming.

Do You Want a Hanging Sleeve?

If you would like to hang your quilt on the wall, or if you might want to enter it into a show, you'll need to add a hanging sleeve to the back. Use the 11" strip you had leftover from making the backing. Most quilt shows require a minimum 3" wide hanging sleeve, so the leftover strip will be more than wide enough. Cut a rectangle 7" inches wide and as long as the width measurement of your quilt. Fold in 1" on both short outside edges, then fold it in half lengthwise. Match the raw edges to the top edge and baste it to the back. Later, you can carefully hand baste the folded edge to the backing layer.

For a professional way to display your quilt, attach a flat sash curtain rod to the wall. The hanging rod can be slipped in between the layers of the sleeve so it will not wear against the quilt backing. The rod ends won't show because the sleeve doesn't extend to the edges of the quilt.

Making the Binding

Binding is the finishing strip of fabric that folds over the outside raw edges of your quilt. Double-fold binding is more durable than single-fold. Binding can be cut on straight or bias grain lines. If your quilt has straight sides and square corners, use binding cut on the straight of grain. Bias cut binding should be used on quilt edges that are curved. For your first quilt, you don't need to deal with the stretchy attributes of bias binding applied to a straight-sided quilt. Later, as you explore more options for finishing your quilts, I'd like to suggest that you read Mimi Dietrich's book, *Happy Endings*, for well-illustrated and comprehensive instructions on a variety of finishing techniques.

Double-fold binding is usually cut 2-1/2" wide. To determine how much fabric you will need, add up the measurements of all four sides of your quilt. Include at least 2" more for turning each corner. The example quilt measures 72-1/2" by 57-1/2", or 260". Add at least 8" for the corners and another 8" to compensate for seam allowances used when joining the strips to make the binding. This brings the total up to 276". Also, include extra binding for the invisible seam finish and the inches lost by cutting the strip ends at a 45-degree angle. I'd be comfortable with at least 290".

Cutting binding on the crosswise fabric grain is more economical than from the lengthwise grain. Since we know that there are approximately 40 usable fabric inches on the crosswise grain, we'll need to divide the anticipated perimeter binding total of 290 by 40 to get 7.25 strips. It's always better to have too much than not enough, so cut eight strips. Since the strips will be 2-1/2" wide, eight strips x 2-1/2" = 20" – you will need to purchase a minimum of 2/3 yard of binding fabric, but it's always reassuring to have a little extra, especially if the fabric isn't cut straight from the bolt, so get a yard.

Prepare the binding fabric as usual: preshrinking (check for color-fastness), drying, ironing, and folding. Remove the selvage edges. With the rotary cutter and ruler, cut eight 2-1/2" strips. Unfold and, using the 45-degree angle line on the ruler, cut off the ends of each strip as shown. All the cuts are slanted in the same direction.

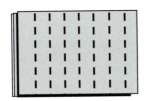 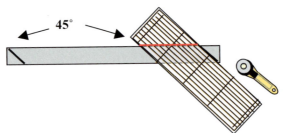

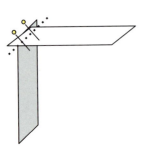

Right sides facing each other, use a 1/4" seam to sew the strips together matching 45-degree angles and offsetting raw edges by 1/4", as shown. Press seam allowances open and trim bunny ears.

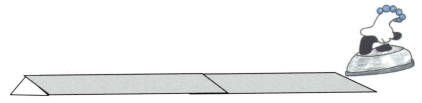

After you make the binding, fold it in half and press, being careful not to let one side drift away from being square to the other. Roll up the binding to make it easier to handle.

Applying the Binding to the Quilt

The width of the seam allowance you use to sew the binding onto your quilt depends on how thick the combined quilt and binding layers are. Let's figure out how wide the seam allowance should be by doing a little test with one end of the prepared binding.

back of quilt

Pin hidden by binding fold

front of quilt

On the back of the quilt, match binding raw edges to quilt raw edges. Measure 1/4" up from the outer edges and place a parallel pin, which represents the future seam. Fold the binding over the raw edges to the front of the quilt making it "full of quilt sandwich." We want the binding fold edge to slightly surpass the line of stitching that will attach the binding to the quilt in order to hide it. If you can't see the shaft of the pin, a 1/4" seam allowance is correct for your application. If you can see the shaft, adjust the seam depth and repin until you find the correct width of your binding seam.

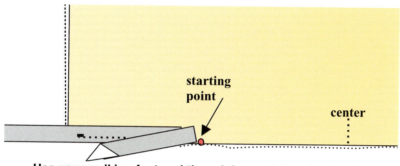

starting point

center

Use your walking foot and thread that matches the binding. Always backstitch at the beginning and ending of seams when applying binding.

Choose a point at the bottom of the quilt back that is halfway between the center and left corner; that will be your starting point for stitching. Leave about 8" of binding unattached, and begin sewing to the quilt using your pre-determined seam allowance. Stop and backstitch at your seam allowance measurement from the left edge. Translation: if your seam allowance is 3/8", stop 3/8" from the left edge of the quilt. Remove the quilt from under the needle.

Turning the Corner: An Automatic Miter

Mitering the binding corners is a cinch. It happens automatically if you follow these instructions:

Fold the binding out and away from the quilt so that its raw edge continues in a straight line with the quilt's raw edge. Place a pin through all layers at the bottom of the quilt. Refold the binding up so that all raw edges are aligned again. Pin this new arrangement in place.

Return the quilt back under the needle and begin stitching at **your** seam allowance measurement from both corner edges; i.e., if your seam allowance is 3/8", then you will begin stitching 3/8" from the bottom and 3/8" in from the left side. Don't forget to backstitch. When we flip the seam allowance to the right side of the quilt, we'll have to tug on it a little, and you don't want the stitching to come out.

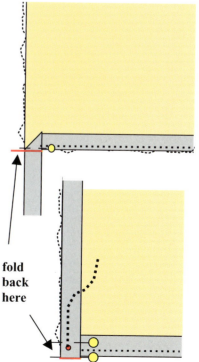

fold back here

Sew all four corners in the same way. When you have turned the last corner and are back to the bottom of your quilt, stop and backstitch about 6" from the right quilt edge.

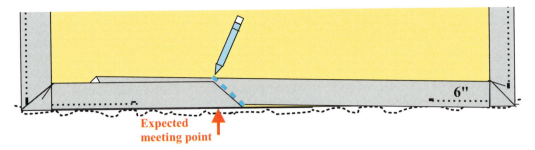

Expected meeting point

6"

If you have too much binding remaining on the right side so that it extends past your original starting point, cut some off. Don't cut it too short; you want to allow the right-hand binding to lie smooth and flat under the left-hand binding. Trace the overlap line of the left-hand binding onto the right-hand binding.

Open the folds of both binding ends. Extend the 45-degree line you drew up onto the other side of the right-hand binding. Using your grid ruler, align and draw a second 45-degree line 1/2" away from the first, making the right binding longer. With the addition of this 1/2", you have compensated for two 1/4" seam allowances needed to join these two ends together.

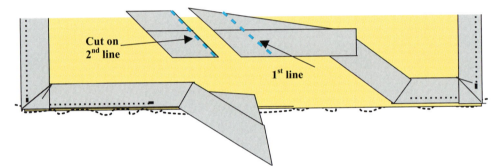

Cut on 2nd line

1st line

Check first to see if your measurements are correct by re-folding the right binding and overlapping the ends again. If the second drawn line is 1/2" past the cut edge of the left binding, go ahead open and cut the right binding on that <u>second</u> line.

Unfold the left binding end. Place both ends right sides together to sew the "invisible" seam. These two pieces will be offset just as they were when you joined the strips to make the binding. After the seam is completed, press it open, trim bunny ears, and return the binding to its original folded formation. Stitch down the remainder of the binding to the quilt. This angled seam will be practically imperceptible unlike overlapped or square-sewn seams. With a steam iron, press the binding away from the quilt on all sides.

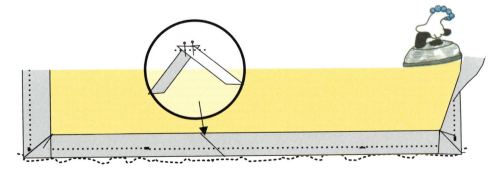

Topstitching the Binding in Place

The binding is sewn to the back of the quilt, so we need to flip it to the front and topstitch it down to finish the edge. We also want to slightly overlap the stitching we just made to hide it. This topstitching should be placed quite close to the fold.

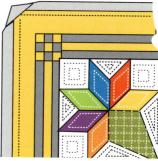

You will see that your binding is curving over the corners of the quilt. This is correct because we put a mitering tuck in each corner. If you feel a bound corner on the back, you'll notice that the little fold created by the miter is turned toward one side. When you hand miter the binding on the front, be sure you tuck that little flap to the opposite side distributing the bulk.

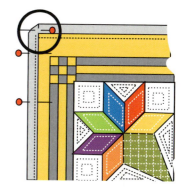

Working on one side and corner at a time, turn the quilt right side up and begin wrapping and pinning the binding over the raw edge hiding the stitching line that sewed it on. About 10" away from the corner, begin to topstitch the binding down with a continuous seam. You will probably need to readjust the wrapped binding as you sew. Backstitch when you reach the quilt edge and remove it from the machine.

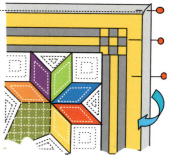

To hand miter the first front corner, fold the binding on the upcoming side over the quilt and the binding you just topstitched. Adjust the back tuck in the opposite direction of the one on the front. Press and pin. You may have to encourage the fold into a 45-degree angle. Continue to topstitch the binding to the second side just as you did the first. Stop with a backstitch at the next edge of the quilt. Repeat this procedure until the binding on all four sides is topstitched down.

To make the corner miters more secure, you can hand stitch them closed, if you like.

Some people prefer to machine sew the binding to the front of the quilt and flip it to the back. Instead of topstitching, they hand stitch the entire binding fold edge in place at the seam line with a blind stitch. I do like this method, but prefer finishing the binding by machine for quilts that will receive a lot of use. The directions given here work for front or back application.

Labels

Quilts are a symbol of someone who cared. People put so much work, time, talent, and love—so much of themselves—into a quilt. Because a quilt is treasured and preserved, it could lovingly be handed down to descendants who may not remember or even know the story of its maker. I hope you will put a label on this and all your quilts to say who you are, where you lived when you made it, the date you made it (or finished it), for whom it was made and why.

Labels are messages written on cloth that are traditionally sewn on the backs of quilts, but you don't have to relegate your information to the back of your quilt. A quilt block that contains writing concerning the quilt of which it is part is called a dedication block and performs the same function as a label. Besides quilting, this is another way to fill up a larger open block patch. If you would like to put a dedication block into your quilt, write the words on it before you sew it in…just in case.

You can find books filled with inspirations for quilt labels and make your own. You can purchase pre-printed labels in packages on the notions wall of your fabric store or quilt shop. There is yardage available printed with a number of labels for you to cut out, fill in, and sew on.

If you have a computer and a printer, making a label is magically easy. You can purchase fabric sheets made to feed through your printer just like paper. You could design a label using all of the different choices your word processing, photo, and graphic programs have to offer. Follow the manufacturer's instructions to print your label. Use the freezer paper technique shown here to sew it to the back of your quilt.

A friend of mine made just such a label. She scanned a photograph of herself holding her grandchild and the lovely pinwheel quilt she made for the little girl. She then printed it onto a special fabric sheet. She cut out the picture, adding an area in which to write information about the quilt and a special message for her granddaughter. What a lovely memento this will be for her little one to treasure for a lifetime.

High-quality, closely woven 100 percent cotton fabric is the best choice for labels. There's just one little trick to remember that will make writing on fabric seem like writing on paper. It involves our versatile friend, freezer paper. On the paper side, draw then cut a square or whatever shape you choose for your label. If you want an irregular shape, draw a mirror image because the shiny side is the right side. Iron the shiny side onto the wrong side of your label fabric, then cut out the fabric adding 1/4" all around.

At this point, I use my computer in a different way to make labels. I choose a font I like, then type the sentiment within the size limitations of my label and print it out on paper. I tape the printed sheet onto my light table, center it, and tape the paper-backed fabric over that, fabric side up. Then I trace the letters onto the fabric. The result looks like hand-done calligraphy, not computer generated print.

You'll need special writing instruments to mark on fabric, which you can find at fabric stores, quilt shops, craft stores and discount stores. They contain permanent pigment color and do not run or wash out. My favorite is archival gel pens. They come in a myriad of shades, so you could add colorful drawings to your labels, if you'd like. Test them on a fabric scrap first.

After your information and any drawings have been placed on your label, peel off the freezer paper. If the paper shape is reversible, like this heart or a square, rectangle, etc., flip it around shiny side up, center it onto the back of your label patch, and pin it in place. Turn the outside fabric edges onto the shiny surface of the freezer paper and iron them to create turned-under seam allowances. You will have to clip curved edges and inverted points. If the shape you chose is not reversible, make a second pattern by flipping the first over and tracing a mirror image onto the paper side of another piece of freezer paper so you can use this technique.

All that is left to do is blind stitch the label to the back of your quilt. Leave the freezer paper attached to your label while you hand sew it on. It will force your needle to the very edge of the patch, helping you make tiny, invisible stitches. When you've only got a few inches to sew before the label is completely stitched on, use a tweezers to pull out the freezer paper template. Tuck the unsewn raw edges back under and stitch the opening closed.

The Blind Stitch

The blind stitch is the most commonly used hand appliqué technique. It is worked from the right to the left, and is fast and easy.

Use a single strand of thread that matches the label patch. Thread and knot your needle and take a stitch under where you want to position the label to secure. Bring the needle up and catch a few threads on the very edge of the label patch. Then take a small stitch through only the backing fabric and up again just under the fold of the patch. Take another small stitch on the patch edge, then another small stitch through the backing, etc. You don't have to pull the full length of the thread through the fabric with every stitch—try after every 3 or 4 stitches. When you have attached the entire patch, make a tiny knot just under the edge of the label and clip the thread.

'Bye for Now ...

I hope you have enjoyed these lessons as much as I have. You have come such a long way in a relatively short period of time, and you have your beautiful quilt to show for it. Let this learning experience be a continuation of the legacy of quilting threaded through time connecting us with our foremothers who made their beautiful quilts mostly for practical reasons, but always with love.

BIBLIOGRAPHY

Beyer, Jinny. Patchwork Patterns. McLean VA: EPM Publications, 1983

Brackman, Barbara. Encyclopedia of Pieced Quilt Patterns. Paducah, KY: American Quilters Society, 1993.

Chalfant-Payne, Suzzy and Susan Aylsworth Murwin. Quick and Easy Patchwork on the Sewing Machine. New York, NY: Dover Publications, Inc., 1979

Cooper, Patricia J. and Norma Bradley Allen. The Quilters – Women and Domestic Art, An Oral History. Lubbock, TX: Texas Tech University Press, 1999

Dietrich, Mimi. Happy Endings. Bothel, WA: That Patchwork Place, 1997

Field, Carol, ed. Better Homes & Gardens 101 Full-Size Quilt Blocks & Borders, Des Moines, IA: Meredith Publishing, 1998

Frager, Dorothy. The Book of Sampler Quilts. Radnor, PA: Chilton Books, 1983

Hassel, Carla, You Can Be a Super Quilter. Radnor, PA: Wallace-Homestead Book Col., 1980

Hinson, Dolores. A Quilter's Companion. New York, NY: Arco Publishing Co., 1978

Leone, Diana and Cindy Walter. Fine Hand Quilting. Iola, WI: Krause Publications, 2000

Malone, Maggie. 120 Patterns for Traditional Patchwork Quilts. New York, NY: Sterling Publishing Co., Inc., 1983

McKim, Ruby. 101 Patchwork Patterns. New York, NY: Dover Publications, Inc., 1962

Mech, Dr. Susan Delaney. Rx for Quilters: Stitcher-Friendly Advice for Every Body. Lafayette, CA: C&T Publications, 2000

Mills, Susan Winter. Illustrated Index to Traditional American Quilt Patterns. New York, NY: Arco Publishing Co., 1980

Poe, Ann. Quilting School. Singapore: Readers Digest Association, Inc., 1994

Quick Method Quilts. Little Rock, AK: Leisure Arts, unknown date.

Reader's Digest Complete Guide to Needlework, Reader's Digest Association, Inc., USA, 1979.

Squire, Helen. Helen's Guide to Quilting in the 21st Century: Hand and Machine Quilting Designs (Dear Helen Series). Paducah, KY: American Quilters Society, 1997.

The Meetin' Place, Quilters Newsletter Magazine, January 1989, Primedia, Inc., Golden, CO.

Verna, Lois, Lofty Decisions, Quilters Newsletter Magazine, November 1999 – December 1999, Primedia, Inc., Golden, CO.

RESOURCES

C&T Publications, Inc.
POB 1456
Lafayette, CA 94549
www.ctpub.com

For rotary cutters and mats:
Olfa Products Group
Division of World Kitchens
1536 Beech St.
Terre Haute, IN 47804
www.olfa.com
1.800.962.OLFA

For Omnigrid Rulers:
PRYM-Dritz USA
Makers of Omnigrid Rulers and Mats
http://1st-sewingsuppliesandnotions.com/index.htm

For X-ACTO Knives and Blades
Bob Corey Associates
Division of BCA Marketing, Inc.
POB 73
Merrick, NY 11566
www.x-actoblades.com
1.516.485.5544

For Wonder Invisible Thread:
YLI Corporation
161 W. Main St.
Rock Hill, SC 29730
www.ylicorp.com
1.800.296.8139
1.803.985.3100
customerservice@ylicorp.com

For cork-backed metal rulers:
Acme United Corp.
1931 Black Rock Turnpike
Fairfield, CT 06432
203.332.7330

Dear Fellow Quilt Teachers
APPENDIX

The information in this book is meant to be shared. I've organized the content exactly the same way my classes are organized. Almost all of the students who have taken my courses finished their quilts, which filled my heart with great pride and respect. Not only did they learn the quiltmakers' skills, they developed confidence in their sewing and artistic abilities. They also gained a new understanding and appreciation of their patience and perseverance.

Permission to make a copy of the templates included in these lessons is granted to the purchaser of each book and extends only to the owner for her personal use. Therefore, when using **The Essential Guide to Practically Perfect Patchwork** as a teaching aid, each member of your class will need to purchase her own copy. Just as you place value on your knowledge and time as a teacher, I place that same value on my knowledge and time that this book represents. We both want to share our love of quilting and encourage others to join us in our treasured hobby in an ethical way reflecting the honorable traditions of our quilting foremothers.

A practical suggestion to you for the timing of each lesson would be a lesson a week for the first six weeks. Take a break of a few weeks before continuing with lessons 7, 8, and 9 giving everyone a chance to catch up and fine-tune. Another break between the 9th and 10th lessons is a good idea to allow the new quiltmakers to finish quilting their quilts. I called the 10th lesson "A Binding Reunion" where we covered applying the binding as well as adding a label to the back of the quilt. This play on words was a light-hearted invitation to all, as during this last lesson we shared treats and compliments on each other's handiwork. We even proudly shared "war stories" about the troubles we had making our quilts.

As a quilting teacher, you know the feeling of sisterhood that sharing your knowledge and skills with your students fosters. It was a surprise to me to learn what an impact teaching quiltmaking had on my students—and on my own life, as a matter of fact.

Happy journeys to all.

1 *The Quilters – Women and Domestic Art, An Oral History*, Texas Tech University Press, 1999, p. 20
2 "Quilter's Newsletter Magazine," January 1989, pp. 14, 54